A Vision for Today
John Eggleston's writings on education

selected by Gillian Klein and
Michael Marland

Trentham Books
Stoke on Trent, UK and Sterling, USA

Trentham Books Limited

Westview House	22883 Quicksilver Drive
734 London Road	Sterling
Oakhill	VA 20166-2012
Stoke on Trent	USA
Staffordshire	
England ST4 5NP	

First published 2004

British Library Cataloguing-in-Publication Data
A catalogue record for this book is available from the British Library

1 85856 301 1

Designed and typeset by Trentham Print Design Ltd., Chester and printed in Great Britain by The Cromwell Press Ltd., Wiltshire.

Thanks to the publishers for permission to use John Eggleston's work.

Contents

A Vision for Today

John Eggleston's writings on education

Introduction

Over a quarter of a century ago, John Eggleston wrote:

> A major part of the study of education is the search for an explanation of its differing responses and outcomes. Why do some students achieve at such markedly different levels from those of others? Why does schooling appear to lead to high adult status for some and the converse for others? Teachers, administrators and researchers have regularly focused their inquiries on the pursuit of the elusive factors that may explain these and a thousand other differences that recur daily in the life of schools and classrooms. The history of education is strewn with accounts of key variables which were believed to embody the explanation of differential educational performance. They have included divine intervention, the inner nature of man, heredity, intelligence, social class, the imperatives of the economic structure and the differential 'constructions of reality' of individuals. (Opening paragraph of *The Ecology of the School* (1977).

The search for explanations continues. We continually need to review and re-consider aspects of our schooling as society develops and as the patterns of working in schools develop hidden changes. The danger is that in focusing on one aspect of education we over isolate that aspect, severing its inter-connections with the rest of schooling.

John Eggleston retained his perceptions of the inter-reliance across schooling of every aspect of education. Consequently his writings, with their humane combination of idealism and realism, are and will for a long time be of significant help in reviewing and planning education policy and practice in the twenty-first century. This selection of work from 1967 to 2001 offers only a brief glimpse of his unfailingly holistic vision of education.

In the years since the major re-formulation of the structure of responsibility for schooling in the Education Act 1944, reviews and re-planning have tended to focus on one aspect of 'now'. But good planning is assisted by considering how we came to where we are, and John's forty years of study, consideration, comparison and sharp analysis will be of help for future years. At a time when 'specialist schools' are being favoured, his analysis of work experience is illuminating. His considerations of curriculum planning are always enlightening, starting with his revision of the school subject of Craft. And as 'inclusiveness' becomes topical, his studies of staying on, of antiracism, and of citizenship education have much to offer. His companion study to the Swann Report of 1985 remains an important analysis of how we can approach racial equality and inclusiveness

One of his deeply significant concepts is of fresh significance: the 'ecology' of the school which is, as he stated 'composed of social, economic, political and ideological components'. John's 1977 study helps us to understand the current situation: the way decision making is distributed In the early twenty-first century, the concerns about resource levels, and the immense differences in the pupil composition of schools and what this will mean for each individual's chances in life.

Our multicultural world and the need for an overall appropriately planned school curriculum is a major challenge in the twenty-first century. John wrote widely and powerfully on this theme, with studies on antiracism, on careers guidance, and on arts education.

In 1993 he chaired the evaluation of the project Arts Education for a Multicultural Society, the report of which was published by Trentham Books in 1995. In this he strongly encouraged 'an active, coherent' approach to arts education which fully incorporates a 'broad heterogeneous curriculum which draws positive advantage from different cultural traditions'.

At his inaugural lecture [as Visiting Professor] at Middlesex University in May 1999, attended by his followers from across

Britain, John tried to bring together the themes of his life and his life's work and locate them in the upcoming curriculum subject of citizenship. Like the sociologist he was, he began with an examination of society and its evolution from agrarian (local), through industrial (national) to technological (global). He wove in the value – to himself and generations of young people – of designing and making things and the inner-directedness earned from succeeding. And he concluded that the 'modest approach to being a citizen' outlined by the government would: 'even if fully delivered in school and elsewhere, be manifestly inadequate for today's society'.

In recent years we have come to reconsider and re-state the importance of educational leadership and in doing so to explore more than before the lives of leaders. John Eggleston's responsibilities and interests ranged from sociology to curriculum planning, from the ecology of the school to the development of the individual's personality, from the crafts to the humanities, from overall school organisation to work experience, and from antiracism to social justice. His project leadership, such as the government's project on the Structure and Function of the Youth Service and the Schools Council's project, Design and Craft Education (1968-1974), was hugely effective and had lasting outcomes. Under his leadership of the Department of Education at the University of Keele he and a team of academics theorised education and led research into teacher training for multicultural society. In the Eggleston report of 1985, he led the companion study to the Swann report and revealed the differential experiences children have at secondary schools depending on their ethnicity. It was not until he was terminally ill that he learned that the Keele team referred to themselves as 'Eggie's Babies'.

His shaping of the Education Department of the University of Warwick enhanced its academic rigour and the quality as well as the extent of staff publications. Both universities gained hugely from his wide-ranging vision and national and international work, from his stringent academic standards and his humane and supportive management style. His energy and enthusiasm never flagged, and they infused his work as an extremely active Visiting Professor at both Middlesex University and the University of Central England. John's lectures, writings, contributions to discussions, and his personal encouragement were much appreciated and greatly influential.

This book is a selection, chronologically arranged, from the range of John Eggleston's exploratory and advisory writing. He wrote 22 books in all, but we have also included chapters from edited collections and journals. The selection opens with a piece on the administrative context of the school then moves to another strand of his work: craft and design in the curriculum, a strand which is brought right up to 2001 in the concluding chapter.

By 1967 John was writing about youth and destinations after school, and chapters 3 and 4 raise issues which he followed up as a Leverhulme Fellow 1994-1997 – see chapter 11. Chapter 5 deals with the sociology of the curriculum and this is followed by a chapter from his seminal book, *The Ecology of the School*. In chapter 7 we return to Work Experience in Secondary Schools and the opening chapter he wrote for the symposium of this title. He followed up these concerns, as we see in chapter 8, now looking especially at how ethnicity factors into work experience, schooling and careers guidance. Never one to duck issues, in the Eggleston Report he reveals the racism that affects young people's schooling and life chances. Chapter 9 is one of his regular contributions to the journal of which he was the Founding Chair of the Editorial Board, *Multicultural Teaching* – an analysis of how the 1988 Education Act suppressed education for equality.

Chapter 10 is taken from the book he wrote in 1992 as the overall volume in a series for students: 'Introduction to Teaching'. In *The Challenge for Teachers*, John speaks intimately to student readers, about themselves and their need to be inner-directed and not other-directed. And he tells them about their pupils and urges them not to mislabel them. His humanity and wisdom are embedded in the deceptively simple writing.

Much is missing. There is nothing from the journal he edited for 21 years, whose title shifted with the development of the subject, to become *Studies in Design Craft and Technology*. Nothing from

Mentoring and Tutoring and little from *Improving Schools*, both journals which he founded and edited for a time.

And there is little about the man. This is not a biography, but we include an abridged CV, which lists some of the many national and international organisations on which John served in Canada, Australia, Europe and the Caribbean. There a very small number of the many tributes to him. And there is, of course, an obituary, one of the many that appeared to mark his passing.

Gillian Klein and Michael Marland
October 2003

1

The Administrative Context
of the School

1967, the main part of a chapter from his book
The Social Context of the School

Since the implementation of the Education Act 1944 *we have continued to consider where decision-making power should lie between central government and the teacher in the classroom, the administrative structure within and beyond the schools, the range of pupils that go to a school, the pupil grouping within a school, and the modes of assessment. Most of these aspects continue to be reviewed and the present pattern challenged – for instance the extent of central government's detailed control. It is very helpful to current consideration to read John Eggleston's 1960s scrutiny on 'potential areas of friction'.*

The changes which modern industrial society brings to the process of education are recurring themes of this volume. Two of these changes are of particular relevance to the administrative context of the school. One is the larger size of the education service – a consequence of longer and more specialised courses in schools and colleges and the associated rise in the numbers of teachers and schools. The other is the growing modernisation of the curriculum and the improvement of teaching techniques in order to ensure an adequate supply of highly trained and adaptable labour for the changing occupation structure with its emphasis on technology. This is a need which is strengthened by the increasing occupational and geographical mobility of parents and teachers, calling for the interchangeability of methods and content of schooling so that diversity of educational practice does not handicap pupils.

The centralisation of educational administration

In consequence, it can be suggested that the focus of professional responsibility is tending to shift from the schools to the local education authority which administers the school. Occasionally a dramatic example of the change is made public by the resignation of a head-master, in protest against 'interference' by the local authority. But for the most part the process occurs without fundamental challenge and is indeed being followed by a parallel process whereby the independent powers of the local authorities are being challenged by central authority. This is a challenge which the central authority has had technical power to make at any time since 1899 as Lester Smith reminds us (Lester Smith, 1964). Yet many observers now claim to detect moves to firmer central control. Alderman Heycock, President of the National Association of Divisional Executives, recently stated:

> Unquestionably during the past few years the Department of Education and Science has assumed firmer control. Sometimes this has been to enforce a national uniform policy as with the scheme for grants to students where local authorities have very little latitude left, or the standardised scheme for determination of free meals where the Minister removed local discretion and imposed a uniform policy. . . . But, possibly, in recent years nothing more demonstrates the increased power of the Department than its control over educational buildings. This has been developed into a code of such immensity and complexity that the freedom of the authority to experiment and of the architect to plan have been seriously curtailed (Heycock, 1965, p78).

Yet another example of centralisation can be seen in the work of the Schools Council, a national body representative of teachers and administrators, which is sponsoring major studies of curriculum development and teaching methods for use in the schools. As with other national research projects, it is intended that the results shall be relevant to all areas. However, in most areas of administration we still have a distinctively local administrative context of schools which demands consideration.

The local administrative context

The influence of the local authority's policy can be seen in many contrasts between different areas – in variations in the provision of nursery school places, in the equipment of primary schools which conditions the pattern of activity in them. The 1944 Education Act gave each authority the responsibility of providing schools in accordance with pupils' age, aptitude and ability; the wide range of provision which was made emphasised many variations between authorities. The era of comprehensive education is again beginning to show the extent of independent local action. The diversity of local schemes of reorganisation is to be seen in *Circular* 10/65 ('Organisation of Secondary Education', 1965). (Interestingly, the issue of the Circular also illustrates an aspect of the growth of central government limitations on local independence.) The 1964 Education Act opens up still further prospects of independent action by the authorities, by permitting them to experiment with the age of transfer between primary and secondary schools. Some of the diversity of local authority provision springs, of course, from the pressure of other variables in environment which are considered in other chapters. A detailed account of the interplay of environmental variables in one area is to be found in 'Going comprehensive – a case study' (Eggleston, 1966).

The policies of the local authority, imposed by their budget, and suggested by their advisory staff, are reinforced by the authority's power to control human resources – to allocate pupils and to appoint teachers to schools. The authority has considerable freedom to distribute pupils in a manner which suits its plans. The power to adjust catchment areas, selective intakes and the numbers of fee-paying places bought in direct grant and independent schools means that an authority can, if it wishes, fill its comprehensive schools and reduce the intake of others. Powers over the numbers and quality of the teaching force can be exercised through the machinery of teacher/ pupil ratios, and the allocation of special responsibility payments.

The concept of 'bureaucracy' applied to educational administration

The policy of the local education authority is exercised directly through the organisational structure of an administrative service which tends to become increasingly professionalised. The pattern of control linking local authority and school is moving nearer to that which is typical of contemporary organisations in commerce and industry. But the bureaucracy of the education service rarely approaches the full rationality implied in the sociologist's concept of *bureaucracy*, with its advanced specialisation, hierarchy of authority, system of rules and impersonality.

Administrative structures in America and England

In both America and in England, the lack of full conformity with the bureaucratic model springs at least partly from the retention and incorporation of local 'amateur' influence. In England there are the elected councillor representatives on the local education committee and the nominated boards of 'lay' school governors. In America there are the elected school boards with responsibility for schooling in areas ranging in size from New York city to tiny rural areas. On both sides of the Atlantic these bodies retain powers of control over the professionals, both administrators and teachers. There are, however, important differences. In England, since 1902, the members of the local education committees have been general purpose representatives, responsible for a whole range of local administration, and generally serving on other committees as well as the education committee. Moreover, their powers are restricted. Important matters, such as teachers' pay and conditions of service and tenure, are a matter for national, not local, government. All the political parties agree to the convention that curriculum and teaching technique should be left to the discretion of the professionals. In America, not only are the elected representatives members of bodies which are solely concerned with education, but also all the matters just referred to fall within their discretion. In consequence, all that the American schools and their teachers do has to be done subject to the approval of lay opinion. The control of education is far more a function of the local community than in England, where there is a more diffuse local and national responsibility. Here, the teacher is effectively isolated from the direct pressures of the community not only because of the differences in administration but also because of his traditional links with external national sources of authority – the universities, the churches, and the central government.

But in both systems it is not only between the lay representatives and the professionals that friction and conflict is likely to arise. It may also occur between the school-based professionals (the head and his assistant teachers) and the office-based professionals (the director of education, his deputy, assistants and advisors). Though of immense importance, little study has been undertaken to examine these potential areas of friction in educational systems. In America some interesting work has been done by Gross on the relationships between the school superintendent (director of education) and both the school board and the teachers in the schools. The study shows some of the considerable problems that arise from the conflicting expectations and obligations to which key figures in administration are exposed (Gross, 1958).

Organisational analysis

An important area of study of educational administration is currently arising out of the application of the analyses of industrial organisational theory to educational organisation. Here the attempt that is being made is to formulate theories of educational organisation which will not only facilitate diagnosis of administrative behaviour but which will also enable the consequences of decisions to be forecast more accurately before they are made and so lead the way to improved administrative practice. We are still a long way from establishing such scientific laws of human behaviour but important preliminary moves have been made by several writers. Perhaps the most notable of these is to be found in *Theory and Research in Administration* (Halpin, 1966).

The consequences of administrative differences

At the moment, however, the evidence available is largely confined to the *consequences* of the administrative regime in which the schools function. Perhaps the most conspicuous of these are the differences in the percentages of pupils entering higher education from the schools of different local education authorities. In 1960 the percentage ranged from 24.9% in Cardiganshire to 5.1% in the Isle of Ely for the counties, from 17.9% in Oxford to 1.7% in West Ham for the County Boroughs. A survey undertaken for the Robbins Committee showed that these variations were not a reflection of differences in ability between the areas, but that they were related to differences in local authority provision and practice. In particular they were significantly related to the number of grammar school places provided by the local authority. In areas where more than 23% of the pupils went to grammar schools, 11% of the whole age group entered higher education. In areas where grammar school entry was low – 18% of the age group or under – only 7.5% entered higher education. The differences remained even though social class variables were held constant. There were also significant correlations between higher education and primary school class size. In local authority areas where primary school classes contained on average over 37.5 Pupils, only 7.7% of the age groups entered higher education, compared with 11.4% in areas where classes contained an average of 32.5 or fewer pupils. In the secondary schools local authority areas which had an average of fewer than twenty pupils per teacher, 11.3 % of the relevant age group were sent to higher education. In comparison, those areas which had a pupil/teacher ratio of more than twenty-three pupils sent only 6.9%. Even within local authority areas there are differences. The Robbins Committee (1963) reported that the West Riding of Yorkshire can be divided into three areas for selective purposes – areas of high, medium or low intake into the selective schools. As might be expected the test requirements for entry into a selective school are highest where the selective entry is lowest. Yet a higher percentage of young people go to higher education from the areas of high and medium intake, suggesting that an important variable is not only the ability of the students at 11 but also the local availability of places in schools which prepare young people to enter higher education.

Clearly the prospects of young people are affected by the administrative arrangements of the local school system in which they happen to be educated, and, in so far as the differences in entry to higher education are not solely reflective of differences in student ability, the policies and practices of the local education authorities can be seen as important factors in the distribution of educational opportunities.

Using the Robbins survey as a basis for calculation, it can be shown that if the numbers of students going forward to higher education from the local authority with the highest total of awards – Cardiganshire – were to be matched by all local authorities the Robbins target for entries to higher education by 1980 would at once be passed, and the United States achievement of 1961 would have been matched (Simon, 1965).

Secondary education and administration

Even more direct consequences of local authority differences are evident when their policies of secondary education are considered. An example arises in studies undertaken by the author in the secondary schooling of seven Midland local education authorities. These showed widespread differences in the provision of selective and non-selective secondary education and, particularly, differences in the provision of extended courses and other opportunities for pupils to stay on after minimum leaving age. These varied from complete discouragement for all but grammar and technical school pupils to generous encouragement and provision for all pupils. In the areas of some of the most 'generous' authorities 'staying on' was a norm accepted by large numbers of pupils, parents and teachers. Yet in the areas of the least generous authorities staying on was not only rare but seldom considered by modern school pupils.

The opportunities for initiative by a local authority may of course be limited by the area it serves. As Chapter 3 has shown, population growth may be insufficient to warrant new building. In such cases new schools and the changes which can go with them can only be introduced by the replacement of existing ones.

The 'downtown' schools in the socially handicapped areas referred to in Chapter 3 bring out such limitations of local authority powers. Authorities are usually obliged to build schools at the same time as the areas they serve are built. In consequence, the child whose home is in the old city or industrial centre often tends to find himself in old, unsatisfactory school buildings. Conversely, the child who lives in the newly-built suburban areas around the large towns is most likely to find himself in a new school and, if he is of secondary age, the suburban child is far more likely to be in a comprehensive school than his peers elsewhere. In the survey of Midland secondary modern schools already referred to, it was found that half the post-war secondary modern schools served predominantly post-war suburban housing areas, and many of the remainder were in semi-rural areas with a considerable amount of post-war housing. On the other hand, two thirds of the pre-1900 modern schools served predominantly Victorian catchment areas, characterised by slum housing, old industrial and mining sites and multi-racial population.

The response of the schools to administrative approval for courses of extended secondary education is illuminating. Predominantly, the response is to provide courses leading to external examinations. At a time when the selective functions of education are largely carried out by means of such examinations, this is an important service for their pupils.

Yet only in a few schools is there regular provision of extended education for those who need 'educational therapy' before examination opportunity becomes meaningful. To some extent this state of affairs arises because, in the local community, an appreciable number of pupils who can be seen to pass recognised examinations tend to bring higher status to the school than an equal number of pupils who are seen to be 'staying on for nothing'. It is difficult and at times impossible for schools or authorities to challenge this kind of community evaluation. Indeed one of the pressing problems of the modern school in the tripartite secondary school system has been the monopolisation of superior local status by the selective schools and one of the few ways to compete open to the modern schools has been through the 'league table' of public examination successes.

The extent to which the examination course dominates the response of the modern schools is none the less surprising. In the enquiry conducted by the author, modern schools were asked to indicate the range of extended courses they offered, including non-examination courses. Only four schools reported non-examination courses yet a check on pupil numbers disclosed that 43 of the schools had 4 or more pupils who were unaccounted for by the examination courses. The non-examination candidate seemed neither worthy of mention nor of special attention in a large number of schools. It has already been noted in Chapter 2 that there are considerable dangers in a situation where the goals of the schools can only be achieved after the end of the basic course of the majority of pupils. In these conditions the majority of pupils can only obtain an incomplete secondary education and an unplanned introduction of extended courses by an authority may result in the distribution of educational opportunity becoming more and not less uneven.

Primary education and administration

Much of what has been said about secondary education is also applicable to the primary sector. Here again there are wide variations in local education authority arrangements which have important consequences for the schools as Appendix 14 in Vol. 2 of the Plowden Report (1967) demonstrates.

However, the primary schools have for many years been faced with a far more explicit administrative task than the secondary schools. They have been required to act in partnership with the authority in the one major selective function which the authority is called upon to administer directly – selection for secondary education. The primary schools have thus found themselves in a unique relationship with the local authority – a partnership in a programme of allocation for the different secondary schools. It is a task which has become more fully centred in the primary schools as greater emphasis is placed on teacher reports rather than test results. It is a task which is still continuing in most local authority areas, including many which, though they have made considerable progress in comprehensive re-organisation, still have selective school places to fill.

The extent to which the primary school has been influenced and conditioned by this task can often be seen. There is the shadow which is cast by the selection tests, usually in English, Arithmetic and 'Intelligence' taken in the final year. It is seen in the distortion of some aspects of the work of the school in face of the tensions and anxieties of the pupils and their teachers who may come to cut down on activities not connected with the test, particularly in areas where concern over the results is greatest. There is little to suggest that the problem is lessened when the authority attempts to hide the test from pupils and their parents. Such an attempt can be seen in this passage from a local authority letter to parents: 'Perhaps your child told you that he was recently given a couple of tests as part of the normal school routine.'

The streaming of the primary schools is closely related to their selective function. By the time the school is due to perform its formal task of selection it may already have effectively sorted out its pupils. By streaming them at the age of seven or eight it will most probably have predicted the results of the eleven plus. More of the A stream children than the B stream children will pass, and there may be considerable surprise if any of the C stream children pass at all. For many years this state of affairs was seen as a sign of the schools' accuracy in allocating children to their 'correct streams'. More recently Douglas in his *The Home and the School* (1964) has shown that streaming can create differences and is, to some extent, a self-justifying process. As we have seen in Chapter 2, children of equal ability at the age of eight who are put into different streams can become different by the age of eleven. The self-justifying process is well indicated in the following statement to the author by the head of a primary school in a working-class urban area:

> The most outstanding feature of this school is that its work is in no way geared to the eleven plus. The majority of the children entering this school are not of grammar school standard, therefore I do not aim to push children to pass the eleven plus. I aim to get through only those children who I know are suited to grammar school life.

References

Department of Education and Science (1965) *Organisation of Secondary Education*, Circular 10/65, HMSO

Douglas, J.W.B. (1964) *The Home and the School*, MacGibbon and Kee

Eggleston, S.J. (1966) 'Going Comprehensive', in *New Society*, 22.12.66

Gross, N. *et. al.* (1958) *Explorations in Role Analysis*, New York, Wiley

Halpin, A.W. (1966) *Theory and Research in Administration*, New York, MacMillan

Heycock, A.L. (1965) 'The Growing Power of the Department', *School Government Chronicle*

Lester Smith, W.O. (1964) *The Government of Education*, Penguin Books

Mason, S.C. (1965) 'The Leicestershire Plan' in McClure, S. (Ed), *Comprehensive Planning*, Councils and Education Press

Plowden Report (1967) *Children and their Primary Schools*, Vols 1 and 2, Central Advisory Council for Education, HMSO

Simon, B. (1965) *Inequalities in Education*, Conference for the Advancement of State Education

2

Crafts in the Curriculum

1971, a chapter entitled 'Craft' in a
symposium edited by Richard Whitfield:
Disciplines of the Curriculum

*At a time when there was what Whitfield called 'our relative and
potentially dangerous neglect of a study of the total curriculum', the
Schools Council had recently been founded (1964) as an independent, government-funded advisory body on internal school
organisation and especially the school curriculum. It published a
huge series of studies, of which* The Whole Curriculum, 14-16 *(on
the committee for which John Eggleston sat) was a major example.
He had an overall interest and skill in curriculum planning. His
own teaching specialism in schools had been 'Craft', and he published major works on this component and was a leader in the
thinking of the range of educational aims that craft teaching can
and should include. This is the main part of his chapter in Whitfield's book, omitting only his inclusion of the objectives set out in
the Schools Council's Research and Development Project in Handicraft (1969). John Eggleston led the way from the narrow, isolated
handicraft courses for boys and girls separately. His vivid des-
criptions of those earlier examples of craft teaching in schools
enables us to understand more fully what has been developed since,
though not always put into practice. His emphasis on thinking is
especially pioneering: his approach, which was to 'identify problems
and test solutions', and his broader vision to include aesthetics and
personal expression.*

11

Man's capacity to modify his environment is still largely determined by his capacity to use three-dimensional materials. Their availability and manipulation are as central to the activities of an advanced industrial economy as they have been to those of any previous social system. Their importance in every phase of human activity from the most basic to the most esoteric is self-evident; their importance in man's capacity to express himself has probably never been so great.

The handling of materials has for many years played an important part in the school curriculum. A number of specially labelled compartments of the timetable offer such opportunities. There are the so-called heavy crafts, involving the working of wood and metal and frequently linked under the somewhat unfortunate label 'handicraft'. This may also involve work with clay, stone, and plastics, which may take place in the wood and metal workshops or in the art and craft studio. (The different title of the location is not without significance for the nature of the activity.) Another branch of the crafts may be seen in applied science and technology, where the emphasis is on the practical exploration of and solution of technological problems in the fields of electronics, engineering, and applied science generally. Here again, the activity may take place in the workshops or it may be based in the science laboratories.

The activities listed so far are traditionally associated with the education of boys, but sex-typing in this area of the curriculum, as elsewhere, is losing its rigidity, and much of the work is now open to girls. Conversely, in the traditional girls' subjects boys may be found with increasing frequency. Here, there are a wide range of activities – basically cookery, needlework, dressmaking, and home maintenance which extend again, in conjunction with the art and science departments of the school, into fields such as interior design, nutrition, and child care. The changing title of this area of craft work indicates this extension: housecraft was renamed domestic science and the collective term now in use is home economics.

In the presecondary school years, work in craft tends to be rather more limited in the range of processes and materials, because of factors such as school resources and the physical strength and maturity of the pupils, though the complex and highly successful activities that are undertaken in the field of junior craft – as it is commonly labelled – often convey very little indication of such limitations. Elsewhere, both in primary and in secondary schools, the proliferation of craft activities is abundant appearing on the time-table under a range of headings, such as rural crafts, gardening, farming, and so on. It is in such extensions as these that the patterns of integration with other subjects of the curriculum, that are such a notable feature of the modern approaches to be discussed later, have their origins.

Craft subjects in the curriculum

It is clear, then, that almost all secondary schools and a number of primary schools have areas of the curriculum given over to the use of three-dimensional materials. In most secondary schools, these take place in expensively equipped rooms with specialist tools and machinery. If only because of the highly specific and permanent nature of the equipment and the rooms in which it is housed, the craft activities undertaken are likely to have a secure place in the curri-culum. Yet much of this activity retains highly traditional emphases and, not infrequently, many parts of the craft curriculum may appear to be more relevant to the nineteenth than to the twentieth century.

In part, this springs from the early origins of the craft subjects. The introduction of manual training and housecraft in the early public elementary schools was very clearly associated with the utilitarian approaches that characterised this sector of education. It was seen as a kind of prevocational training for the rapidly growing ranks of semiskilled and domestic workers. This utilitarian justification was largely responsible for the introduction of the subject in the 1880s in the technical and trade schools, into the higher grade schools in the 1890s, and into the senior forms of the elementary schools in the early years of the present century. The incorporation of manual train-ing and housecraft into the grammar schools after 1902 was again largely on predominantly vocational grounds as the recruitment of pupils for such courses up to 1944 included many who left to enter the trades and other manual callings – though the recreational as-pects of the crafts were often realised for the able junior pupils. The carpentry and housecraft instructors were not unknown in the independent schools, too. There are reports of their activities here as early as the end of the nineteenth century. Occasionally, their presence was in response to the enlightened enthusiasm of a reformist head or possibly in indirect recognition of the teachings of William Morris; more often it was so that the dull child should not be entirely unable to use his hands should ill luck fall his way.

The rather low status of the crafts subjects that tended to arise from this state of affairs was somewhat reinforced by the specialised – even deviant – background of the craft teacher in the secondary school staff. Their expertise was specialist and definable; clearly recognised and yet of a kind unshared by their colleagues. Their training was also different, usually involving industrial or trade experience or, at the very least, attendance at a specialist college. The craft specialists often became something of a respected isolate in the school. Their colleagues seldom visited their distant workshop or housecraft: centre, and found communication difficult when they did; even the headmaster often found himself beyond his range and went infrequently, if at all. The pupils recognised that they were people apart – the boys gasped as, time after time, the master's joints fitted to perfection – the girls knew that the mistress's cake would never fail to rise. Yet, this isolation, coupled with the status problems of the work, inhibited the process of integration, and often tended to limit its educational significance, rather than enable crafts to be an important influence in the total curriculum.

Developments in craft teaching

Yet the craft specialists have always endeavoured to offer more than their vocational and utilitarian specialism. They have regularly sought to play a part in the development of such matters as technological understanding and aesthetic judgement through the use of materials. They have consistently claimed a part in the transmission of values as well as of knowledge and skill, and have sought to develop a range of socially approved value orientations in their pupils. These have frequently emphasised the 'traditional manual working-class values' – at least in so far as they can be known by the teacher. They have tended to include respect for work and workmanship, the dignity of labour, honesty and integrity in the use of techniques and materials. A recurring feature has been the avoidance of the short-cut – encouraging the more difficult long-term solution, rather than the easy temporal response (the back of the cooker is always to be cleaned; the underside of the table is always to be sanded if not even polished). Yet value orientations of this nature were never the whole story. Consistent efforts to develop standards of taste, appreciation of the quality of line, texture, form and function, and much else, have been regularly and increasingly in evidence in teaching of the craft subjects. Improved courses of initial training and in-service education for craft teachers have greatly facilitated these efforts in recent years. The introduction of work for the BEd degree in home economics, art, and handicraft has encouraged the development of analysis and research in relevant fields, and a new research-orientated journal *Studies in Design Education and Craft* [edited by John Eggleston – eds.] is now published.

With their established position in the curriculum, and their concern for both vocational and moral education, the specialists in craft were well placed to participate in the era of curriculum developments that began in the 'sixties. The impetus for modification and adaptation that influenced other subjects was clearly relevant for the crafts, too. The changing technological and economic organisation of work, domestic life, and leisure had obvious implications for craft; new tools, materials, and processes threw many of the traditional activities of the craft curriculum into sharper relief. Activities, such as the hand-planing of timber, the 'basic ingredients only' regime in cookery, the emphasis on hand rather than machine laundry, and much else, were thrown. into question. The need to consider the role of craft education in new types of schools – sixth form colleges and middle schools – and to examine its relevance for new categories of pupils, notably those who will remain to 16 compulsorily after the raising of the school leaving age led to further reappraisals by individual teachers and the various specialist organisations in this field. The Schools Council sponsored a research project in applied science and technology (Project Technology) based at the Loughborough College of Education and, more centrally in the craft field., a research and development project in handicraft based at the University of Keele. Both projects have now produced preliminary reports (see references). A research study has also been initiated at Goldsmiths' College, London, in the field of art and craft education for 8–12-year-old pupils, and preliminary studies have been undertaken in the art and craft and the home economics field – both with special reference to the raising of the school leaving age.

All this has led to a fundamental reappraisal of the objectives of craft education. A central feature of the new approaches that are emerging is that the traditional emphasis on doing and making are joined by a parallel emphasis on thinking. This springs from a growing realisation that education is no longer predominantly an exercise in remembering either knowledge or skills. In the recent past, the ability to reproduce was a central element in the performance of adult roles. But increasingly the capacity to remember and replicate even the most complex processes is being taken over by non-human devices and the distinctive human role in work, domestic life, and in leisure becomes much more concerned with the capacity to adapt, to initiate, and to modify; in short, to solve problems which very frequently are in three-dimensional form. In this connection, it is interesting to remember that one of the important consequences of the space programme has been the mechanisation of a range of high-precision processes that previously were only capable of being performed by highly skilled hand labour.

All this has particular relevance to the curriculum in craft. It calls for the establishment of opportunities to identify problems and explore and test solutions in a range of technological activities, and here the work of project technology is of central importance. But it also has a general vocational relevance in that the kind of skilled work undertaken by ordinary young men and women is likely to lie far less in the traditional trades and skills. More and more, it is likely to rest in the maintenance, adaptation, and servicing of a range of domestic, office, automobile, and industrial equipment. Here, in the workshop, in the kitchen, even in the mobile service unit, they will certainly be undertaking skilled activities, but they will also be performing diagnostic and creative roles. Opportunities to experience work of this nature are being introduced very widely in workshops and home economics departments in many secondary schools, and this provides ready links with other areas of the school curriculum in that they are concerned not only with practical activities but with a range of associated fields of knowledge and understanding in science, mathematics, English and most other subjects. Such activities may be associated with work experience situations in factories, schools, and offices, sometimes in liaison with colleges of further education.

But problem-solving in three-dimensional materials is not confined to work situations – it is of great importance in the domestic environment. The widespread enthusiasm for the enhancement of the home and its equipment that characterises our society offers obvious areas of development for the curriculum in craft. The range of activities now open to the young man and woman setting up home, through the development of new techniques and materials, is one that has much significance for the craft subjects. New materials for decorating, plumbing, upholstery, roofing, floor covering, are being introduced in the craft curriculum – their properties analysed, their applications explored, all in practical situations. Associated with this may be the analyses of cost, quality, availability, and the appraisal of aesthetic qualities. Here again, practical test situations may be set up.

Crafts subjects in the context of the community

At this point, we have moved close to another central area of the craft curriculum – that which is concerned with the development of personal expression. In our consideration of the home environment, we are, in fact, considering one of the key areas of personal expression in contemporary society. The possibilities for development in this field are abundant. One example is the planning of gardens., one of the most promising areas of personal expression available to young men and women in our society, yet all too frequently the realisation of this potential is limited. The clothes post in the middle, the straight row of concrete slabs leading to it and lawns of equal size on either side are still the predictable end product of the experience for many adults. Programmes in the craft subjects are exploring alternative ways of undertaking garden planning and development, and in doing so are transforming an often traditional approach to school gardening in the process. One important part of such projects is to assist pupils to undertake the relevant skilled work more effectively, so that, for instance, the gnomes do not get frosted and the terraces do not subside. But the central activity is again the thinking one – the identification of possible problems and their successful solutions that may facilitate fuller achievement and more satisfying personal expression.

In this and in all aspects of the work in craft subjects is an underlying objective – the development of thinking that leads to an ability to contract in to the decision-making processes that determine the environment of the individual whether it be in work, at home, or elsewhere. The craft subjects do not stop at the execution of individual schemes, but aim to equip young people to enter into meaningful dialogue with others who are determining or modifying the environment – such as the architect, the building society official, and the housing officer. So projects on the home will go on to explore the activities of these persons and will, for example, examine the ways in which a building society conducts a survey, the way in which a builder plans a 'private development', the way in which the local authority determines the area of discretion that its council house tenants are allowed, and so on. In this way, craft subjects will be making a contribution to pupils' ability to take part in the decision-making processes about their environments, rather than taking a passive or accepting role.

Parallel schemes are being developed in the field of leisure activity. Projects on entertaining, on karting, or land yachting, for example, are designed to enable pupils to participate personally not only in the relevant technical or physical expression, but also in the individual aesthetic expression that increasingly characterises leisure activity – from the adornment of scooters to the customisation of cars. Here there is still great opportunity for the craft specialist: when one studies the way in which young people adorn their clothes or their scooters or their motor cars, it is apparent that so far the craft subjects have not always been able to have a major impact in helping them to achieve such forms of expression. The new enthusiasm to bring the work of the craft subjects more fully into line with the culture and values of contemporary society, to develop with it rather than apart from it, seem likely to change this situation.

The craft subjects are not only concerned with the expression and participation of the individual, important as this is; they are also concerned with aspects of school and community service. Some schools are working with geriatric units and pupils are preparing equipment that augments the resources provided by the Health Service, others are preparing play equipment in educational priority areas, while others are undertaking child care and welfare schemes, and the skills and understanding needed to carry them out are often found in crafts subjects. In other schemes, the craft subjects may play a major part, as, for instance, in the restoration work being undertaken at Fountains Abbey. Here, schools are involved in a number of replacement projects in wrought-iron and stone. This work is far nearer to the traditional activities of the craft subjects, but in a community context that opens up a range of decision-making processes and relationships. A number of conservation schemes are also springing from the work of the craft workshops and departments. In yet other schools, all the craft departments are collaborating in a school service project: a sixth form centre, which is based upon a caravan, is being built in the metalwork department, this is being fitted out in the woodworking and home economics departments and decorated in the art and craft studios.

The value of the problem-solving approach

Characterising all these approaches is the problem-solving situation where problems are identified, solutions explored, and results tested. This process goes under many names; it is the engineering design line of project technology; it is the design process of the art studio; it is the product-testing of the home economist. This similarity is leading to a new collective identity for the craft subjects – which are becoming known as the design subjects. The move to reorganise the craft subjects into design departments is taking place rapidly in schools up and down the country and bringing a new unity to this area of the curriculum. Not only does it offer a far more coherent basis for integrated craft activities, but it also serves to identify the nature of pupils' achievements in this area, bringing together intellectual, expressive, and practical approaches in a unified enterprise. It also emphasises that the new trends in craft education are building upon rather than replacing traditional ones. The skilled manipulation of materials is still of considerable importance, and in many areas is being augmented with new skills, such as those needed for the handling of new textiles, instant foods, specialised paints, concrete, ceramic tiles, plastic plumbing units, power equipment, and much else. But this development of skill is closely associated with that of intellectual and expressive approaches. The intellectual aspects are now seen as a part of the practical activities, as well as being essential preludes and conclusions, while the expressive component has become far less an intuitive and non-articulated aspect, but instead one that can be rationally examined: like the intellectual aspects, it is now seen as a component that is never absent from any of the activities of the craft subjects.

One of the important features of the craft subjects is that they are able to offer this range of intellectual, aesthetic, and practical activities to a wide range of pupils, and this is especially so in that they allow an opportunity for intellectual activity to many pupils who, because of their lack of verbal competence, are unable to acquire this in many other areas of the school curriculum. In the craft subjects, there is the opportunity for non-verbal communication through materials – with teachers who themselves are able to communicate with the pupils in this manner. Its importance has been recognised more fully as we have come to realise the extent and the consequences of verbal handicap, where social as well as physical problems present fundamental difficulties to the child in the language used by the teachers and in the books being used. Headteachers have always recognised this to some extent, as is shown by their enthusiasm to offer the craft teacher large periods of time with the difficult and inarticulate senior and low stream pupils. The full educational significance of the relationship implied by these decisions is only now being seen clearly.

An important feature of these new developments in craft education is that they involve a change not only in the nature of the craft activities and the thinking and feeling associated with them, but also in the roles of the teachers and pupils. The outcomes of the problem-solving approaches are not known in advance; if they are, then the approaches are but a confidence trick. There is no question of the teacher 'knowing the right answer'; this can only arise from the relationship between pupils and the teacher. The teacher indeed brings specialist knowledge and experience, as he always has done, but, in addition, he does much more. He is also a learner, and as Bruner has reminded us 'when the teacher becomes a learner then his teaching takes on a new quality'.

The future

It is likely that the new approaches in the crafts may provide bases for new and potentially valuable integrations within the total curriculum, and may do so while still retaining the same excitement and enthusiasm that work with materials has always been able to offer at its best. What is more, it is likely that it may be able to offer a genuinely comprehensive set of educational opportunities wherein pupils of all abilities can achieve a full measure of success that is intellectual and aesthetic, as well as practical. The new approaches in craft education are unlikely, however, to lead to a new orthodoxy of approach in the way that the old schemes of work in craft attempted to do. Instead, it is likely that the very creativity, inventiveness, and discovery that have been the goals of craft education specialists for so long will increasingly come to characterise not only the work of the pupils, but also the very organisation of the curriculum and teaching.

References

Schools Council (1966) *A Schools Approach to Technology,* Schools Council Bulletin No. 2, HMSO

Schools Council (1969) *Education Through the Use of Materials,* Schools Council Working Paper No. 26, Evans/Methuen

3

A Youth and Community Service for the Future

1976, from *Adolescence and Community, the Youth Service in Britain*, Chapter 10

Between 1968 and 1974 John Eggleston led a country-wide research project on 'the organisation and purpose of the Youth and Community Service in England and Wales', which had been commissioned by the then Department of Education and Science. He vividly evoked what he called 'the heart of the service – responsiveness and caring for the needs of the individual in an open and unstructured way', stressing that 'Youth has been of major concern to the adult population of all known societies'. He and his team started by finding: 'Our initial reaction after the first month of exploratory field work was one of astonishment, even bewilderment'. This was caused partly by the fact that the 'myriad members, workers, youth officers, management committee members and the vast periphery of other 'involved people' seemed at first glance to lack pattern and structure', and yet 'careful observation indicated recurrent patterns of purposeful and intense activity'. In Chapter 10 of his book John summed up the then 'present situation', covering structure, values, membership, and the aims of members. He then offered this analysis of 'Ways Forward', which still speaks to those in education and the youth service today.

Ways Forward

The evidence of the study suggests that, increasingly, the main thrust of the Youth Service would lie in the development of the participative identity through which the young may achieve meaningful adult roles in the sort of society in which they are likely to live; a society of which most of them are well aware and willing to accept if the community will accept them.

There is little doubt that the fundamental issues are to do with power – its availability and distribution – and are political in nature. Of course they always have been, the new feature is that they are now somewhat more explicit and often more urgent than before. To date, the experimental organisations seem to have been more successful in providing such facilities particularly for those most lacking in social and political power, but there is no reason why most existing youth organisations could not adapt to make an even more effective contribution to this end. There is indeed considerable recognition that they can (Davidson, 1973). And in those parts of the service that are linked closely to the schools, the new school curriculum approaches in community involvement and the development of individual judgement are capable of offering important reinforcement.

But it may well be that in focusing on this area the Service may wish, or even need, to place less emphasis on some existing areas of provision. The concept of the Youth Service as being able to provide most things for most young people is possibly something of an anachronism. It may be that we no longer need to try to serve the needs of, say, many of the young people who are successful and well catered for in schools.

It may also be that the Service need not try to replicate in its clubs those facilities that appear to be better provided commercially, especially when the commercial provision is not only more flexible and popular but also self-supporting while that of the Youth Service is less popular and subsidised. Instead it may be that the major focus of activity needs to be for those who need the service most, identifying, like the schools, 'Youth Service priority areas' that pinpoint where effort shall be concentrated. In doing this we may well find that we can also develop what is at present a somewhat uneven professionalism in the Service, offering improvements not only in the sheer expertise of providing the new kinds of activities we wish to provide, but also in areas such as counselling and guidance and the range of social work skills that are probably most helpful in the development of identity and participation, particularly for those in greatest need.

What forms may such a Youth Community service take in the future? To answer this question we must go beyond our evidence into the field of speculation – though it is speculation guided by five years of intensive experience of the service gained during the production of this report. Our surmises may be set out as follows:

The continuance of a considerable amount of existing 'mainstream' provision. There is little doubt that many of the existing 'purpose built' voluntary organisations will survive largely intact with only gradual modifications of their programmes and values. Here we include the uniformed bodies, the church organisations and the other predominantly voluntary bodies with an established identity that satisfy long standing needs of substantial groups of young people. It is clear that there will also be a continuing need for many of the more successful general purpose clubs and organisations that can provide relaxed, relatively undemanding leisure activities and a social meeting ground at an acceptably mature level for young people for whom alternative facilities are unavailable because of cost or distance or simply indifference.

But beyond this continuing core of voluntary and statutory provision, and in part springing from it, we might expect to see the bifurcation of the predominantly general purpose provision into two forms:

1. Junior clubs predominantly for those at school providing a range of activities appropriate for the fourteen to sixteen age range using, in the main, the facilities of the school campus and recognising, instead. of denying, the links between school and Youth Service provision, links that already exist in the growing similarity between school and 'club' curricula and methodology. Our evidence, like that of Bone and Ross (1972), suggests that young people of this age keenly wish to use the Service and that their needs are clearly different from those of older adolescents. It could well be that attendance at the club, like attendance at the

link course in the college of further education, could be seen as an appropriate 'school attendance' by the 15 year old 'ROSLA', children providing an acceptable alternative to the full scale continuation of formal schooling and an alleviation of the problems often associated with this group in the schools.

2. A gradual running down of specific 'segregated' provision for older adolescents. Some provision is already occurring in the context of community and leisure centres where the young are joined by adults in activity-focussed programmes. But for the majority it is arguable that general purpose recreational activities can often not only be better provided by commercial organisations that are well structured yet highly flexible, but also that such provision is increasingly accessible and acceptable to a majority of older adolescents. It may even be that appropriate arrangements could be made to subsidize participation in such commercially provided leisure by adolescents who are unable, on economic grounds, to finance themselves. Such an arrangement, though unprecedented in the Service, has precedents elsewhere in the social services and may well be a considerably less costly facility than the widespread and often under-used current provision for older adolescents within the Service.

The further development of largely short term, exploratory 'non-established' predominantly local projects of varying size and scale for young people 'in need', those experiencing social, economic and physical difficulty. The experience of the late 60s and early 70s of a wide range of national and local initiatives such as Community Industry, Community Service Volunteers, YVFF and many others has indicated the general viability and relevance of such projects – a viability and relevance that may be enhanced in the later 70s with improved training and local coordination and guidance.

A number of developments of this kind could well fall within the context of the Government proposals for a national Community Development Project involving experiments in community development in selected areas of high social need which envisage a 'co-ordinated approach by an inter-service team to the total personal needs of individuals and families and of the community as a whole'. Yet it is interesting that, in the list of 'relevant services' that follow the proposals, the Youth Service is one of the few services that is not included in the 'inter-service team' suggested for each area. Clearly the potential role of the Youth Service in such fundamental proposals for community welfare has by no means been fully recognised; this is also the case in other areas such as the development of Inter-mediate Treatment strategies. Our suggestions for improved training and more effective local supervision and co-ordination may hasten such recognition.

The further development of special interest groups with open membership but with special opportunity for participation by young people of 'Youth Service age'. These include at one end of the spectrum the groups concerned with matters such as sport, archaeo-logy, railway preservation, theatre, music and the like, to those concerned with pressure groups for community action both at the national level such as Shelter, Release and Child Poverty Action and at the more spontaneous local level in play groups, claimants' unions and so forth. There is abundant evidence of the demand for parti-cipation in such activities from young people of all levels of society. The well known report (DOE, 1972) of the 50 Million Volunteers working party offers some indication of the potential support for activities in the area of community action, conservation and welfare. In a revised Service it may well be that ways might be found to provide appropriate financial support on a broader and more regular basis than now to such organisations. Again the recommendations of 50 Million Volunteers are relevant. As has been suggested, such a service may well be less formalized, less permanent more client determined, and in consequence more responsive than many of the present arrangements often are. It may even be possible for it to be-come both less expensive and more effective at the same time. Certainly such a revised service might minimise some of the weak-nesses that arise from the present efforts to try to do too much over too wide an area. The Youth Service, like its members, needs to achieve identity and status in contemporary society; to become politically and professionally mature. A sharper focus may offer considerable assistance in reaching these goals.

How may we evaluate the kind of Youth and Community Service that might spring, in the late 1970s, from the evidence we have considered? The question of evaluation is indeed central to the service – as we have seen, it lies at the heart of almost all the difficulties, conflicts and uncertainties. Yet the very process of evaluation is itself surrounded by conflict. One school of thought appears to say 'if you cannot measure it, it's not worth doing', its opponents appear to claim 'if you can measure it, it's too trivial to be worthwhile.'

In practice evaluation is in part a consequence of the culture of the evaluator; sociologists of the phenomenological school show us that our perceptions and interpretations of social situations – our view of what is 'really happening' – may be determined by the way our social background has led us to 'understand' what we see. Is then the whole process of evaluation a subjective one, unamenable to any statement of general principle or practice? Our experience within the five years of the project suggests that such a conclusion, though in part true, is not a necessary one. There appear to be a number of questions that one can apply to contemporary practice in the Service; and though these questions may not be researchable ones, they are certainly ones that can be answered with considerable clarity by any competent, sensitive practitioner. They are, in our view, unquestionably more important that records of buildings, attendance, parades and fund raising. These questions appear to us to include:

1. Do young people join and leave the organisation or the club when they are ready to and, in particular, is care taken to ensure that they are not held back from reaching the latter stage?

2. Similarly are projects, activities and programmes initiated and continued because there is evidence that they are serving a useful purpose for members or the community or both and not primarily because they are keeping the organisation in being or the workers in work?

3. Is the provision of a kind that could not have been available to the members at all or only with considerable hardship without the Youth and Community Service, rather than just replicating in a more conveniently available form other public and commercial provisions?

4. Is the initiative and motivation increasingly springing from the minds of the members or those they are serving and is the adult worker not in the driving seat for the whole time? Are the outcomes unpredictable because the spontaneity or initiative of the members cannot be foreseen rather than wholly predictable because of the adults' capacity to manipulate the situation?

5. Has the experience of the Service effectively brought members into relationships with adults in the community as equals or near equals and not caused them to be labelled or even to label themselves as segregated and different? Are community issues seen as differences of ideas rather than differences between young and old?

6. Finally, and perhaps most fundamentally, has the existence of Youth and Community Service provision led members to achieve and experience power; to develop judgement in its use and understanding of its nature and to construct or reconstruct their own self-image in the process?

Our experience suggests that these questions are often implicit in general evaluations – for example in Hart's evaluation of YVFF: 'We see real value in this sort of very different field work and we think it's good value for money (quoted in Moorehead, 1974).

We are of the opinion that where all or most of the questions can be answered in the affirmative with regard to any specific aspect of Youth and Community Service provision then it is likely to be right and proper for some branch of the Service to be there and to be in receipt of public funds for the purpose. The evidence of our report suggests that there are many such cases and that there will be many more in the kind of future Youth and Community Services we have considered – a future in which, however integrated and co-ordinated our diagnosis and responses become, there are likely still to be clearly identifiable 'youth' needs and a Youth Service. Yet however certain the need, it is equally certain that discussion, debate and controversy about the way it is to be met will continue, as the DES Discussion Paper (1975) has recognised. We hoped that the information assembled in this report will be of continuing assistance in the debate.

References

Davidson, C. (1973) *Last but not Least: essentials for a creative community service in Liverpool*, Liverpool Council of Social Services

Department of the Environment (1972) *50 Million Volunteers*, Report of the 50 million Volunteers Working Party, HMSO

Department of Education and Science (1975) *Provision for Youth*, DES

Moorhead, C. (1974) 'Helping People to Help Themselves', in *The Times*, 8th April

4

Administrative and Community Variables in Staying on at School

1967, from *Some Environmental Correlates of Extended Education in England*, published in the journal *Comparative Education*, 3(2), March 1967, and reprinted in the symposium *Contemporary Research in the Sociology of Education*, 1974

The question of why so many pupils leave earlier than is educationally desirable has long been a major British question, and it clearly links with the structural organisation and admission arrangements of separate schools, the internal pupil organisation, and the characteristics of the pupils' backgrounds. The post-war ambition of the Education Act 1944 included raising the legal school-leaving age from fourteen to sixteen. In the 1950s, surprisingly perhaps, little attention was paid to this. The government's Central Advisory Committee's report of 1954 (Early Leaving) focused only on the drop-out from selective grammar schools. The 1944 legislation was phased in by raising the leaving age to fifteen in 1944, but it did not rise to 16 until as late as 1972, thus retaining 60% more of the age group. By the late fifties worries were increasing as such a large proportion of pupils were still leaving early and very many without qualifications. A number of sociologists, teachers, and other educationalists were stressing the relationship between school leaving and family class background. John Eggleston started a five-year study in 1958. The correlations he found in the eight Local Education Authorities are still relevant today, especially in the light of the current consideration of school organisation and pupil selection.

Some environmental correlates of extended secondary education in England

One of the major tasks of the English educational system since 1945 has been to supply increasing numbers of highly educated recruits to the labour force. As in other major industrial societies this has presented problems of expanding the provision of higher education. But a particular problem in England has been the pattern of state secondary schooling. In the selective 'tripartite' arrangement which has characterised the English state system since 1945, only the 20-30 per cent of students admitted to the selective grammar or technical schools have generally had the opportunity of an education which, in content or duration, could lead to entry to higher education. The majority of students who entered the secondary modern schools followed programmes which terminated at the minimum school leaving age and which were specifically precluded from leading to qualifications which could secure access to higher education. For all but the minority the minimum school leaving age marked the maximum extent of full time education, and the ensuing limitation of life chances.

Both the Crowther Committee, reporting in 1959, and the Robbins Committee, reporting in 1963 were able to demonstrate that the expansion of higher education in England was being handicapped by twin shortcomings of the secondary school system. One was a failure to mobilise sufficient recruits, the other, seen as a consequence of the selective procedures employed at eleven plus and after, was a failure to mobilise all of the most able recruits.

One beginning of current moves against the restrictive assumptions of ability implicit in selective secondary schooling arose during the 1950s in the secondary modern schools. A number of these schools contrived to run programmes after minimum leaving age leading to qualifications which were passports to pre-university and professional courses. They found that increasing numbers of their students were able to complete such programmes successfully. In 1954 only

5.7 per cent of all. secondary modern pupils remained after minimum leaving age, in 1963 20.7 per cent did so. A primary motivation of many teachers and administrators in these moves was to challenge, on behalf of their pupils, the class linked selective procedures of the tripartite system. In the late 1950s this was a challenge which could be backed by the findings of the empirical studies of English sociologists. The expansion of numbers eligible for higher education was only a by-product, though an important one, of such moves. More recent moves to replace tripartism by non-selective comprehensive secondary schooling can still be seen to spring from similar motivations by teachers and administrators. Yet the prospect of expanding the numbers of eligible recruits for higher education presented by the comprehensive school is striking, for a common feature of all schemes of comprehensive reorganisation is a more open access to extended secondary education by all students.

The expansion of opportunity for access to extended secondary education suggested the need for examination of the circumstances in which student decisions to stay on occurred. The need for such study is underlined by the associated phenomenon – the relative decline of the selective grammar and technical schools. These schools have an 'institutionalised' holding power over their pupils until at least sixteen, for it is expected without question that all their pupils will complete a five-year course. and in fact nowadays virtually all of them conform. In the 'open' comprehensive situation decisions to stay on can be made at the minimum leaving age of fifteen, not at eleven.[1] Moreover they tend to be made far more by the individual pupil and less by the school. In consequence the predictability of decision is lessened.

Opportunities for the writer to visit a number of comprehensive and secondary modern schools in England brought an awareness of marked variations in decisions to stay on by students in different areas and in different types of school. This suggested that some predictive factors may be identified in the *external* environment of the schools, notably the socio-economic status of their catchment areas. But a further cluster of environmental variables seemed to lie in the local administration of education – the availability of places in comprehensive schools; the equipment and facilities of schools; and the postleaving age programmes offered.

Accordingly a study was planned which would examine two areas of variables external to secondary schools: those associated with the administrative regimes in which the schools operated and those associated with their catchment areas. The hypotheses for the first area were that a high incidence of staying on at modern and comprehensive schools would be associated with high standards of buildings and equipment; wen-developed programmes of extended courses and successful examination results therein; comprehensive rather than tripartite secondary schooling; low intakes to selective schools where they exist, and larger rather than smaller schools. The hypothesis for the second was that a high incidence of staying on would be associated with catchment areas where pupils came from homes of predominantly high socio-economic status.

The research was conducted in a representative group of eight English local education authority areas – the county boroughs of Burton-on-Trent, Coventry, Derby, Leicester and Nottingham and the county councils of Derbyshire (south and south-east division), Leicestershire and Staffordshire – over a five year period, 1958-63. Though as befits its representative nature, this area was still predominantly served by tripartite secondary schools, it contained two of the long-established areas of comprehensive school provision in England, the Coventry and Leicestershire comprehensive schools. Additionally it contained examples of two of the many variations of the tripartite system, the Nottingham bilateral schools and the special secondary school transfer. arrangements at Derby.

Three indicators of staying on were established and applied to all 'non-selective' schools in the area (240 modern and bilateral secondary schools and 20 comprehensive schools). These indicators were as follows:

(a) Extent of staying on after fifteen (minimum leaving age) in the survey period, expressed as a percentage of the total 14 year old age cohort in the school in the previous year.

(b) Extent of staying on after sixteen (to enter a fifth year of schooling) in the survey period, expressed as a percentage of the total 14 year old age cohort in the school two years previously.

(c) Change in the rate of staying on in the school during the survey period.

A list of administrative and socio-economic variables was subsequently drawn up for investigation in the schools. The final list of variables was as follows:

1   Sex of pupils.

2   Size of school.

3   Intake of pupils to selection schools from the non-selective school catchment areas.

4   The extent of staying on after sixteen in selective schools drawing pupils from the non-selective school catchment areas.

5   Material environment of the schools. This was a ranking of the specialist teaching facilities available in each school undertaken on similar lines to the survey reported in the 'Newsom Report'. In each case the ranking was undertaken by two independent assessors, the few differences being resolved by investigation of the school by the writer.

6   Age of school building. Again following Newsom precedent, schools were asked to report the approximate date of the construction of the earliest part of the school buildings in current use.

7   Provision of extended courses. After preliminary investigation it was decided that the most useful inventory of courses was as follows:

  i   Courses leading to GCE O level exams.

  ii   Courses leading to other external examinations usually taken at the end of the fourth year of school, such as those of the College of Preceptors or the Royal Society of Arts.

  iii   Courses leading to local education authority examinations held at the end of the fourth year, such as the Coventry Education Authority's Pre-Technical and Pre-Commercial Certificate. (Non-examination extended courses were almost non-existent.)

8   Success rates in GCE examinations taken in the fifth year of extended courses.

9   Success rates in examinations taken in the fourth year of extended courses.

10 Socio-economic status of the catchment area. This was established by applying the Juror Index[2] to the total population of the catchment area of each school.

Examination of these variables for each school was undertaken with the aid of school, local education authority and electoral records and the generous assistance of teachers, administrators and electoral officers is acknowledged. On completion, this data and that for the three indicators of staying on was coded and correlated and analysed along lines similar to those suggested by McKennell.

The survey area
Administrative variables
Not surprisingly the most highly significant correlations are those between staying on and the provision of identified extended courses; indeed this provision and the factors associated with it emerged as being of overriding importance in the incidence of staying on. ...

This evidence, though negative, none the less refuted the common suggestion that a high selective intake drained off the able pupils who would otherwise remain in the modern schools and take extended courses. However, the situation seemed to require further investigation, as the evidence obtained made no allowance for the way in which staying on in the modern schools might be affected by the overall approach of the local authorities to the provision of secondary education. As has been mentioned, the group of eight local authorities under investigation contained some authorities which were unrepresentative in their secondary school provision (Coventry, Leicestershire, Nottingham and Derby).

Did these modifications to tripartite provision mask some of the relationship between the selective and modern schools' staying on figures which might occur in a 'conventional' local authority?

In an attempt to examine this secondary hypothesis some of the data for these 'conventional' authorities with almost entirely tripartite

TABLE 1. Administrative variables and staying on. Bilateral and secondary modern schools. Product moment correlation coefficients *(r)*

Variable	Staying on after 15	Staying on after 16	Rate of change in staying on
School size*	0.2846	0.3571	0.2175
Intake of selective* schools in same area	0.0511	0.0021	0.0297
Staying on after 16 in selective schools in same area*	0.0720	0.0906	0.0783
School material environment*	0.3086	0.1507	0.1829
Age of school buildings*	0.2844	0.1244	0.1607
Extended course provision†	0.6525	0.6341	0.4180
GCE exam success†	0.5375	0.5409	0.3859
Non-GCE exam successes†	0.4495	0.2890	0.4495

* Variables examined for 240 schools Variables examined for 125 schools (all schools in Coventry, Derby, SE

† Derbyshire, Leicester, Leicestershire and Nottingham).

TABLE 2. Administrative variables and staying on. 115 secondary modern schools in 'conventionally' organised areas. Product moment correlation coefficients *(r)*

Variable	Staying on after 15	Staying on after 16	Rate of change in staying on
School size	0.1485	0.2382	0.2284
Intake of selective schools in same Area	0.1785	0.1976	0.1075
Staying on after 16 in selective schools in same area	0.3535	0.1806	0.0997
School material environment	0.3024	0.1628	0.1660
Age of school buildings	0.2916	0.0543	0.0858

provision of secondary schooling was isolated and correlated with the three indicators of staying on (Burton-on-Trent, south Derbyshire and Staffordshire. Only three isolated comprehensive schools existed in these areas during the survey period). The correlation matrix for the 115 modern schools of these authorities is set out in Table 2.

In most respects the pattern of correlation is similar. School size is significantly correlated to staying on after sixteen and to change in the rate of staying on, though not to staying on after fifteen. As before, the condition of school buildings and the age of the school is significantly related to staying on after fifteen at the 1 per cent level but not significantly related to staying on after sixteen. The most notable change is in the relationship of the variables associated with the selective secondary schools. In these conventionally organised authorities, staying on in the modern schools after sixteen emerged as being significantly and positively correlated to the selective school intake and, just, significantly and positively correlated with staying on after fifteen. Moreover the correlation between staying on after sixteen in selective schools and staying on after fifteen in modern schools is highly significant. These figures were substantiated by reciprocal correlations for the schools in the 'non-conventional' areas.

The evidence indicates that, in 'conventional' authorities, a high rate of entry to selective schools is associated with a high rate of staying on in the non-selective schools, and in turn suggests that the effective demand for extended education is not tied to a limited supply of pupils who can benefit from it, but rather is a demand which grows with the growth of educational opportunity. It may be that the situation was masked in 'reorganisation' areas, not only by the provision of comprehensive schools, but also by location of such schools and the transfer arrangements associated with them – matters which are discussed subsequently.

It was not possible to subject the comprehensive schools to the same correlation analysis as the modern and bilateral, as they were not distinct in their administrative variables. All came into the largest categories of schools size; all had superior material environments and buildings; all had a full range of extended courses, and all shared a level of examination successes midway between those of the selective schools and the modern schools. Table 3 is presented, however, and indicates that staying on in the groups of comprehensive schools in Leicestershire and Coventry was of a higher order than the aggregate rate of staying on in the whole remaining tripartite area (grammar, technical and modern schools) of the same two authorities.

TABLE 3: Percentage of pupils remaining after minimum leaving age in comprehensive and tripartite schools (Coventry and Leicestershire)

1964	Comprehensive schools*	Tripartite schools
Coventry	57.6	39.3
Leicestershire	49.2	33.4

* Only comprehensive schools established on or before September 1958 (Coventry) or September, 1960 (Leicestershire) are included.

Socio-economic status

The Juror Index was applied to the 125 bilateral and modern schools in Coventry, Derby, Leicester, Nottingham, Leicestershire and south-east Derbyshire. The correlation between the Index and the three indicators of staying on is shown in Table 4.

TABLE 4: Juror Index and staying on. 125 bilateral and secondary modern schools. Product moment correlation coefficients *(r)*

Variable	Staying on after 15	Staying on after 16	Rate of change in staying on
Juror Index	0.1964	0.2509	0.1414

The correlations are significant at the 1 per cent level for staying, on after sixteen but only at the 5 per cent level for staying on to fifteen. The correlation with change in the rate of staying on just fails to reach the 5 per cent level of significance. The stronger direct relationship with the external environment of the pupil at sixteen plus would.seem to be a corrolary of the diminished force of the school environment (buildings and facilities) noted previously at this age. The relationship between staying on and socio-economic status in the comprehensive and bilateral schools of Coventry, Leicestershire and Nottingham is of interest. Inspection of the Juror Indices of the catchment areas of these schools reveals not only a close relationship between socio-economic status and staying on, but also a relationship between the socio-economic status of the community and the provision of comprehensive or bilateral education. The relationship is shown in Table 5. (For Coventry and Nottingham the catchment area assessed for socio-economic status is that from which both selected and non-selected pupils attend the school, not the extended catchment for selected entry.)

TABLE 5: Socio-economic status of school catchment area*

	Coventry	Leicestershire	Nottingham
Average JI of comprehensive, Leicestershire Plan orbilateral school catchment area	25.31	19.8	15.46
Average JI of modern school catchment area	20.25	13.17	9.22

*   Averages are not weighted and are therefore approximate, particularly in Leicestershire where there is a wider variation in size of school. However, as the average size of comprehensive, Plan and bilateral schools is greater than that of the modern schools, the inaccuracy underestimates the difference in J1 of the two sets of schools.

The table indicates that the reorganised secondary schools are characterised by catchment areas of superior socio-economic status in each regime.

In view of the relationship between socio-economic status and staying on shown in Table IV, the previously demonstrated success of these schools in holding their senior pupils seems less impressive. Does then the main advantage of the comprehensive type of secondary school lie not in its comprehensiveness but in its superior catchment area.

In an attempt to examine the situation more fully the Juror Indices for all the schools in Coventry and Nottingham were correlated for each area, with the indices of staying on. The results are shown in Table 6.

TABLE 6: Juror Index and staying on in Coventry and Nottingham. Product moment correlation coefficients (r)

Variable	Staying on after15	Staying on after 16	Rate of change in staying on
JI Coventry(N=22)	0.4293	0.2125	0.2993
JI Nottingham(N=32)	0.3018	0.2784	0.2178

The figures show that for both authorities the correlation between the JI and the three indicators of staying on for all schools is less than for the aggregate of schools shown in Table 4. (The actual number of *(r)* is of course higher in each position because of the far smaller number of cases.) The situation seems to be that though the majority of the schools are situated in areas of relatively superior socio-economic status, their influence is none the less to lessen the link between staying on and socio-economic status found in the secondary modern schools. This could in part result from the achievements in holding-power of the few comprehensive and bi-lateral schools in the lower socio-economic areas. But it also springs from the superior holding-power in the remaining modern schools in the area of reorganisation, as compared with the modern schools in non-reorganised areas. The incidence of staying on in the modern schools of Coventry, Leicestershire and Nottingham was higher than that for all other authorities in the survey area (other variables held constant).

The link between high socio-economic areas and comprehensive versions of secondary education is an almost inescapable one for local education authorities. Clearly the authorities are under obliga-tion to build new schools in response to rapid population growth – a particular problem in Coventry and Leicestershire. If the authority has adopted a policy of comprehensive education then it is logical that these new schools be comprehensive schools and equally logical to build them in the new housing areas where the demand exists. These new areas, whether of private or council housing, tend to be areas of high socioeconomic status. Moreover they may contain the only large sites which are suitable for comprehensive schools in the authority's area. From the authority's viewpoint the building of com-prehensive schools in these areas also avoids the difficulties of dis-turbance of other schools, especially if the new comprehensive schools are used as neighbourhood schools. And the policy of neigh-bourhood schools is often forced on the authority by the very rapidity of the growth of the child population in the new areas of the suburbs. In such circumstances the children from the old city centres are faced with multiple handicaps in their access to the comprehen-sive schools. Thus schools which may be designed to act as instru-ments of egalitarianism can, in many cases, only achieve it indirectly by the creation of a climate of educational expectation which spreads over from the comprehensive into the modern schools still serving the predominantly lower socio-economic areas.

[John Eggleston goes on here to sum up the then current plans in Leicestershire, Coventry, Nottingham and Derby, before concluding:]

Summary

An examination of staying on beyond minimum leaving age in English non-selective secondary schools of eight representative English local education authorities was undertaken, to explore hypotheses that voluntary extension of schooling is associated with identifiable administrative and community variables in the school environment.

Optimum conditions for student decisions in favour of extended secondary schooling were, as hypothesised, the availability of successful examination courses (virtually no non-examination courses existed) in large schools with superior material environment and with catchment areas of superior socio-economic status. Student response was greater where provision was available in the school community where they received their initial secondary education; concentration of provision into a few schools by transfer arrangements inhibited response, though the inhibition was less in superior areas.

The hypothesis that low intakes to selective schools would be associated with high rates of staying on in the non-selective schools serving the same catchment areas was not substantiated. In the survey area as a whole there was no significant correlation. But in the 'conventional' areas of secondary provision the hypothesis was reversed – a high intake to selective schools was positively and significantly correlated with a high rate of staying on in the nonselective schools. Moreover high rates of staying on in both types of school were positively correlated.

Comprehensive systems emerged as being superior to tripartite systems in the provision and holding-power of their extended courses. (There was however, some evidence of less complete holding-power of the comprehensive schools over their most able pupils than would have been expected in a tripartite system.) The overall superior holding power of these schools seemed largely to be accounted for by the superior socio-economic status of their catchment areas. But the opportunity for extended education within all schools seemed to be a feature of local authority areas where comprehensive provision existed; so that staying on even in their modern schools with inferior socio-economic catchment areas was of a higher order than in schools with similar areas elsewhere.

The examination of the hypotheses was followed by consideration of the prospect of extended education at a time of relative decline of the selective schools with their institutionalised holding power and their replacement by 'open' comprehensive systems with broader social and intellectual intakes. It was hypothesised that the school adolescent community could, in certain circumstances, act as a countervailing force to 'dropping-out' at minimum leaving age.

Notes

1 By the time of this study the youngest school leaving age had been raised to 15. His point about pupil decisions also applies to specialist choices, hence the relevance to 'Specialist Schools'.

2 At that time (until 1963) there was a property qualification for service as a juror, the occupation of a dwelling with a rateable value of £20 per annum or more, and the proportion of the population thus qualified to be jurors was seen as a measure of social and economic status.

References

Beloe Committee (1960) *Secondary School Examinations other than GCE,* Secondary Schools Examination Council.

Crowther Report, volume 1 (1959) volume 2 (1960) Central Advisory Council for Education.

McKenell, A.C. (?) 'Correlational Analysis of social survey data', in *Sociological Review*, issue 13, p.157.

Newsom Report (1963) *Half Our Future,* Central Advisory Council for Education.

Robins Report (1963) *The Demand for Places in Higher Education*, Committee on Higher Education.

5

Sociology and the Curriculum

1977, the first chapter of his book
The Sociology of the School Curriculum

Curriculum planning is one of the most difficult educational tasks. It has only rarely been considered coherently in all its aspects. During his years as Head of the Department of Education at Keele University, John Eggleston further developed his analytic approach to the whole breadth and depth of the school curriculum, stressing:

> *Though the curriculum is being subjected to extensive scrutiny, there has been little specifically sociological examination; socio-logical approaches to the curriculum have tended to be narrow, concerned with limited areas, or to have been based on a single ideological perspective.*

He said that 'This book has taken a long time in the writing', and in it he brought together a wide range of thinkers with his own clear approach and his specialist sociological focus.

What is considered to be 'knowledge' in a society? Equally importantly, what is regarded as 'non-knowledge'? In most societies with schools one of the best places to look for answers to these questions is in the curricula used in the class-rooms. Here we can find not only many examples of the knowledge that is socially approved but also some of the 'legitimating ideologies' that lie behind it.

The diversity of patterns of approved knowledge was early noted by Mannheim who in *Ideology and Utopia* asked:

> How is it possible that identical human thought processes concerned with the same world produce different conceptions of that world? . . . Is it not possible that the thought processes which are involved here are not at all identical? May it not be found, when one has examined all the possibilities of human thought, that there are numerous alternative patterns which can be followed?

There are many examples of fundamental differences in thought processes. North American Indians have, for the most part, no way of saying 'why' in the characteristic manner of the North American whites. For them the crucial question in the consideration of events is 'how did it happen?'. The difference is fundamental. For the Indian, knowledge is the accumulation of material that is believed to be explanatory. For the white, knowledge is the accumulation of answers that are believed to be rational.

Knowledge and culture

Differences in thought processes and the differences in the perception of events that ensue lead to differences in the store of knowledge possessed by each society and by each group. These stores of knowledge transmitted from generation to generation with only gradual modification form the *culture* of societies and groups. Indeed it is culture that identifies not only societies but also tribes, nations, races, social classes and most of the other semi-permanent groups of social life. Components of culture may include attitudes to one's fellow men in and out of the group, appropriate perceptions of the economic system, dietary restrictions, work ethics, religious and political beliefs as well as a whole series of what Schutz (1967) has called *recipe book knowledge* consisting mainly of rule-of-thumb formulae which can be applied in a routine way to everyday situations. Culture with its basis of stored, shared, valid and legitimate knowledge constitutes the accepted way of life in a group. The learning and internalisation of at least an essential core of the culture by each individual is seen to be an essential prelude to achieving a recognised adult identity or, as Durkheim puts it, 'to construct the social being'. It may also be necessary for the individual to learn variations of the culture or *sub-cultures* – stores of knowledge that are required, over and above the common culture, in order to achieve full membership of a group such as a student society, a youth club or a school staffroom. Such knowledge may include understanding the subtleties of dress, the acquisition of 'in speech' and the learning of approved work norms. Structures of sub-cultural groups such as Dennis, Henriques and Slaughter's (1957) study of a mining community show clearly how sharply different are the sub-cultural definitions of knowledge between different communities and how rigidly these definitions are maintained – between, for example, the definition of men's work and women's work. The relationship between the shared perceptions of knowledge and individual behaviour are at the heart of the definition of culture and sub-culture.

Transmission and legitimation

But in both culture and sub-culture it is important to identify not only the knowledge content but the ways in which it is defined at any given moment as valid, correct, proper and generally unquestionable – in other words as being *legitimate*.

All societies have processes not only to ensure the storage and transmission of knowledge but also to make certain that its definition becomes internalised by the young. In pre-industrial societies such processes were conducted by church, community and family. These institutions transmitted appropriate religious beliefs, stratification principles, agrarian and military skills, procreational and child-rearing practices; often holding an initiation ceremony to mark the successful transmission of the most central aspects of the knowledge. In industrial societies such *socialisation* came to require supplementations.

The increasing complexity of knowledge needed by all members literacy and numeracy – in order to perform adult occupational roles occurred at a time when the strength of church and community was diminished by migration to the new industrial areas. But the problems of industrialisation were not confined to the transmission and legitimation of occupational knowledge. The movement to the towns, through weakening the strength of the socialisation of the established communities, weakened the hold of community definitions of knowledge such as consensus norms of living together, definitions of differences, rights and responsibilities, the rule of law and much else. Moreover, new definitions appropriate to the mass society rather than to the local community were called for. To achieve all this the school and its curriculum were called upon to become an essential instrument in the transmission and legitimation of knowledge in the industrial society. In short, to become instruments of social control that help to ensure the maintenance of the social system – its knowledge, its status, stratification and above all its power.

Distribution and evaluation of knowledge

Yet knowledge is not only defined, transmitted and legitimated in all societies, it is also distributed. Every society makes different amounts and kinds of knowledge available to different categories of members. Some areas of knowledge may be sacred or private and careful selection may take place before access to them is allowed (Bernstein, 1975). Still other areas may allow the exercise of great power when possessed and here there may be rules to determine the struggle to attain them. Furthermore, knowledge is evaluated; medical and legal knowledge is characteristically accorded high status; manual skills. especially of a routine nature, are usually accorded lower status as are those who exercise them. The distribution of knowledge is also a feature of sub-cultures as the study by Dennis, Henriques and Slaughter (1957) clearly showed. Patrol leaders in scouting attend separate courses from ordinary scouts to receive knowledge that is not available to ordinary scouts; head-teachers receive information from local education administrators that cannot be divulged to ordinary teachers. Their power is re-defined or reinforced in consequence.

In all these matters the school curriculum takes on major responsibilities. As Musgrave (1972) has noted, 'curriculum stands analytically at the centre of the process whereby any society manages its stock of knowledge'. The distribution aspects of the school curriculum are amongst its most obvious characteristics – different curricula being available not only to children of different age and sex but also to those for whom teachers attribute differences in ability, prospects or propensity to use knowledge. The judgments made by teachers in this and all other aspects of curriculum must themselves of course be seen in the context of the definition of knowledge within the society in which they teach and the professional sub-cultures of which they are members.

Curriculum studies

Yet despite such abundant justification for a sociological study of the curriculum, until recently there has been remarkably little attention given to the curriculum by sociologists, who have tended to take it as a 'given' feature of the school systems they have studied in their investigations of socialisation, differential opportunity and class-room interaction. The early encouragement of Mannheim for a sociology of education based upon the sociology of knowledge was not taken up.

The rapid development of 'curriculum studies' and 'curriculum theory' that can be seen throughout the contemporary literature of education has arisen from other, predominantly non-sociological, sources. It springs, in the main, from the large-scale programmes of re-examination, renewal and revision of the school curriculum currently taking place on the initiatives of teachers, local education authorities, professional organisations and sponsoring bodies such as Schools Council and the Nuffield Foundation. Such programmes have commonly responded to pressing needs in the schools, most notably in the secondary schools faced with such problems as comprehensive reorganisation and the raising of the school-leaving age. But the apparent redefinition of many areas of curriculum knowledge has also been a factor for change. It is argued that the content of scientific knowledge changes in an age of electronics; the content of mathematics changes in an age of computers; the content of language changes in an age of mass communication. Associated with these changes in the definition of content there are also believed to be changes in the appropriate distribution of knowledge to the individual. In the recent past it was believed that the curriculum should 'stock up' the individual with appropriate knowledge (facts, skills and values) that would stand him in good stead throughout the adult life anticipated for him. This was a belief based upon the assumption that adult roles changed only slowly and the knowledge needs of existing generations of adults could therefore be used as a reasonable guide to the requirements of the emergent generations. Many educators assert that, in contemporary society, not only does knowledge appear to change more rapidly but also that there are more efficient and less costly methods of storing it than in the memory of the individual. In consequence, the emphasis of curriculum is seen to shift to the individual as a knowledge developer and user rather than as a walking storage system. The educator's objectives for his curriculum tend to be expressed increasingly in terms not of remembering but of creating, discovering, and inventing. Such approaches implicitly – yet seldom explicitly – seem to suggest that the social control function of the curriculum is being diminished, that instead individual determination is being fostered along the lines of the Durkheimian shift from 'mechanical' to 'organic' social solidarity.

Yet despite the unmistakable sociological assumptions associated with these and many other views of curriculum and their widespread endorsement by teachers, both the practice and the 'theoretical developments' that have sprung from them have been for the most part devoid of sociological analysis. In consequence the study of the curriculum has usually lacked an adequate consideration of either the social factors that influence it or the social implications to which it gives rise both within the school and in the society at large. Many of the so-called models of curriculum change in particular imply a set of sociological assumptions that are surprisingly naive. Some imply a degree of consensus concerning aims of the curriculum that, even amongst teachers, is patently untrue. Still others imply a possibility of curriculum change merely through the manipulation of content and methodology. With such. a slender basis of sociological analysis the possible consequences and even the very feasibility of new curriculum approaches can only be incompletely examined as was clearly to be seen in the first Open University curriculum units *The Curriculum: Context Design and Development* (1972). The somewhat greater sociological content in the revised course is reflected in the two course readers (Harris, Lawn and Prescott, 1976, and Goldby, Greenwald and West, 1976).

Sociological initiatives

It is not difficult to find reasons for these omissions by sociologists. For many years their preoccupation with selective processes gave rise to a situation in which the content of the curriculum was largely ignored (even though the differentiation of pupils was often seen to be achieved through differentiated curricula).

But in more recent years the situation has changed very rapidly. A number of sociologists have produced papers that review the areas in which a sociological perspective may be applied to the study of what is taught in schools. In consequence the curriculum has come to be seen more clearly as an important instrument, if not the most important instrument, in the process whereby the school helps the young to assume adult roles. More importantly, the curriculum is also viewed as a central factor in the establishment and maintenance of the power and authority structures both of the society and the school. In consequence sociologists have become interested not only in curriculum content, method and evaluation, but also in the origins and support of the implicit and explicit values that are embodied in the curriculum. They are interested in how the curriculum is legitimated, in why decisions, both overt and covert, are made as they are and in the social factors that determine the choice of subjects and their content and method. As Bernstein (1971) has put it, the sociologist now wishes to explore the ways in which a society selects, classifies, transmits and evaluates its 'public' knowledge. This brings us to the heart of the matter – the view of the school curriculum as one of the important instruments through which the prevailing features of a society's cultural system are carried; wherein its knowledge is transmitted and evaluated.

This new interest of sociologists in the curriculum is of course closely linked with the renewed interest in the sociology of knowledge itself. Here particular attention centres on the renewed emphasis that the nature of knowledge is not fixed and unalterable but rather a consequence of the perceptions of individuals. These further moves from a positivist view of knowledge to a reflexive one open up highly interesting questions concerning the legitimation of knowledge and in particular the legitimation of the curriculum. Alongside these new approaches there have also been sociological explorations of curriculum ideologies and decision-making procedures and some valuable work on the classification of curricula. Information on the history of both 'traditional' and 'progressive' curricula has also become more fully available and alongside this case studies on the processes of 'curriculum innovation' have been undertaken.

References

Bernstein, B.B. (1971) 'On the Classification and Framing of Educational Knowledge', in Young. M.F.D. (Ed), *Knowledge and Control,* Collier-Macmillan.

Bernstein, B.B., (1975) vol. 3, p. 82, 'Changes in the Coding of Educational Transmissions on the Curriculum', in *Class, Codes and Control*, Routledge and Kegan Paul.

Dennis, N., Henriques, F.M., and Slaughter, C. (1957) *Coal in Our Life*, Eyre and Spottiswoode.

Goldby, M., Greenwald, J., and West, R. (Eds) (date?) *Curriculum Design and Development,* Croom Helm.

Harris, A., Lawn M., and Prescott, W. (Eds) (1976) *Curriculum Innovation*, Croom Helm.

Mannheim, K. (1936) *Ideology and Utopia: An Introduction to the Sociology of Knowledge*, Routledge and Kegan Paul.

Musgrave, P.W. (1972) 'Social Factors Affecting the Curriculum', in P.W. Hughes (Ed.), *The Teacher's Role in Curriculum Design*, Angus and Richardson.

Open University (1972) *The Curriculum: Context Design and Development*, E283, Units 1-12, OU Press.

Schutz, A. (1967) *Collected Papers*, Vol. 1, Martinus Nuijhoff, the Hague

6

Micro-ecology:
The School and the Classroom
as an Environment

Throughout his years of teaching, John Eggleston engaged with the puzzle of educational provision: why is it that schools with similar intakes serve their pupils so differently. In a book which he saw as one of the important titles in his canon, he used the concept of ecology to analyse the factors that shape learning and teaching in schools and the complex interconnections between them.

This collection opened with the first paragraph of the book: The Ecology of the School *(1977). Choosing an extract was difficult, but we settled on taking it from his chapter: 'Micro-ecology: the school and the classroom as an environment'. Never was his prescience more apparent – his discussion of one school's campaigns (p64-6 in this volume) foreshadows the dilemmas in the now-statutory subject of Citizenship education.*

For most people the dominant feature of the ecology of education is the school. It is a feature that impinges most strongly on their consciousness, involving them inescapably for some of the most formative years of their lives. The experience of it influences much of what happens to them throughout their lives; their perception of education as a whole is crucially determined by it. For the education service too the school is its focal point. It is here that by far the greatest concentration of resources is assembled – it is the core of educational provision to which all education that precedes it is preparatory and all that follows is consequential.

The whole of this book is about the school. Its dominance is so great that it constitutes almost the totality of the educational ecology of the majority of human beings. Only the minority transport themselves to the protected sub-ecologies provided by the universities, polytechnics, colleges and adult education classes. And even for this minority the route is essentially through the school system, responding to the resources that are devoted to its creation and maintenance. For a few, a somewhat greater control over the resources available to them in the school system may be obtained by a purchase of places in independent or private schools; for the majority the realities of the public distribution of resources for schooling constitute the personal reality of their educational environment.

But the schools are not only the central core of the ecology of education; what happens in them also helps to determine that ecology. Inevitably much of the ecology of the school, as we have seen, is decided outside its walls by committees and associations of a variety of individuals who have a view about the appropriate nature of schools in the social conditions in which they exist. But power, manifest or latent, also rests within the school. The ways in which the school uses its resources, makes them available to or withholds them from the students and the strategies by which it influences the future availability of resources are as important as any of the processes we have considered so far. In this chapter we shall examine them in greater detail.

How the school distributes its resources

Sometimes schools feel powerless to control their input of resources. Teachers may feel that 'the new school may never be built', that there are perennial shortages of books, stationery, laboratory equipment and all other necessary material resources. Requests for alleviation may appear to sink without trace into the bureaucracy of the local education office. Yet, in practice, all schools enjoy substantial discretion in the allocation of a substantial supply of resources to different categories of students. There are many decisions that have to be taken within the school – selecting examination classes, the distribution of teaching roles, the distribution of access to laboratories, workshops and other specialist facilities. Schools vary in the extent to which they may exercise discretion in varying the categories of resources they receive. Almost all have some choice in deciding which books they shall receive from funds earmarked for book purchase, which laboratory equipment they shall receive from their equipment allocation. Other schools may have the discretion to buy more or fewer books in a system of *virement* wherein money can be switched from books to science equipment or games equipment and vice versa. The extent of *virement* varies between local authorities but most limit this by specifying 'minimum standards of equipment' in various areas of the school. Much rarer is the possibility of virement between materials and staff salaries, though Briault (1974) does indicate a prospect of virement between teaching and non-teaching staff:

Schools and colleges differ very widely in the curriculum they provide and in the ways in which they set about the task of providing learning opportunities for their pupils or their students. In some schools there may be a readiness to use nonpersonal learning resources of wide variety; in others there may be an unwillingness to do so. There should, therefore, be the opportunity within the school to consider not only how it should expend its capitation in terms of materials and equipment, but also to consider that expenditure in relation to the expenditure on non-teaching staff and on teachers. For example, each school should have to consider extensions of its curriculum or the provision of very small teaching groups against the demand that such arrangements make, not simply on teaching staff, but on total resources. The school would then be in a position to recognise and to take decisions about its needs on the one hand for more teachers to provide greater variety in the curriculum (to staff new 'A' level subjects for example), and its desire on the other hand to improve its clerical and librarian support in the library or its technician support in the science field or the field of educational technology.

But of even greater importance is the belief in *professional autonomy* which is now being espoused by many individual classroom teachers. It is a view which sees the teacher in control of the situation in the classroom. It is he who decides what is taking place and his decisions are a consequence of his professional judgement. He may exercise it in terms of his understanding of child development, his understanding of the needs of individual pupils or even his grasp of the fundamental nature of knowledge itself and the way it should be presented and made available to different categories of students. Acting in these ways his professional judgement is backed by his professional and academic training. This model of professional 'sovereignty' is seen to be to some extent modified by a few external constraints, but even these may be of diminishing significance. The examination system appears to be being brought under the control of teachers through Mode 3 strategies and teacher-dominated advisory panels. HMI and local Inspectors become translated to Advisers, while the introduction of more democratic patterns of school management tend to diminish the overriding power of the head. Curriculum development, with its emphasis on diversity, spontaneity and the ensuing choice by the individual teacher from a wide range of options, in any case makes it difficult for the head, or even the head of a department to oversee the work of the teacher in the detailed way that was possible when the curricular options open to him were both more restricted and more predictable.

Whilst the view of teacher autonomy unquestionably exceeds reality in many schools, it is in its existence of far greater importance than the actual consequences in the day to day life of the classroom. It represents a new dimension in the dynamics of power in the school, articulating a claim by the classroom teacher for a larger and more effective voice in the allocation of resources in the school for materials and for non-teaching assistants to enable him to do the things that as a professional teacher he believes are necessary for the children he teaches.

Yet although the claim for voice in the distribution of resources may appear to be individualised and even spontaneous it is not difficult to pick out a pattern of ideological positions which are adopted by many teachers. These are global positions which, like the political party ideologies that we have seen in our consideration of the local authorities, are general rather than specific, continuing rather than episodic.

Two main ideologies may be identified, broadly labelled traditional and progressive. Vaughan and Archer (1971) have emphasised the long term nature of ideologies of these kinds; what is of more recent date is their institutionalisation and reification. Traditional orientations to an allocation of resources suitable for established forms of school organisation, curriculum and teaching methods had seldom needed an articulated written defence until the development of a well documented progressive/radical alternative orientation. Such a stage occurred in the 1960s and it was at about this time that the various movements for the maintenance of traditional standards came into existence and adopted written as well as spoken forms of advocacy. Notable British examples were the Black Papers and the Campaign for Educational Standards. Eggleston (1973) has set out a detailed comparison of the two ideological positions and their use in the schools. On the one hand there is the traditional orientation which emphasises commitment to long established forms of learning, standards, institutions and value systems. The progressive orientation on the other hand espouses new understandings, new socially relevant studies, multi-purpose flexible institutions, contractual relationships and a more open distribution of knowledge – essentially a view of resource allocation and response that emphasises the personal perspective of teachers. Though both orientations are widespread, often occurring within the same school, analysis suggests that there are clear indications of a gradual but unmistakable move from the traditional to the progressive ideology with unmistakable consequences for the allocation of resources. It is a view of the school, its resources and its power structure, that has close connections with the Durkheimian concept of symbolic order rather than with the Weberian concept of structure.

Resources and social control

Although the distribution of resources in school reflects both the ideologies and the power structure that exist in the school, the manner in which it is undertaken has central implications for the distribution of power in society. The availability or non- availability of teaching or other resources to a student can critically determine his own opportunities to exercise power as an adult. The selection, identification and distribution of those to whom such opportunities are given by the schools will, to a large measure, decide the social structure and the distribution of power in the future society. It is argued by writers such as Bowles and Gintis (1977) that the major objective in the allocation of resources in the schools within the education system is to ensure the continuation of the existing social system by distributing and using resources in such a way as to create the 'right numbers' of people holding 'the right skills and values' for the needs of the economic system. In short the task of the schools is seen to be to preserve the social ecology intact by acting as instruments of social control.

There is some evidence that suggests that the distribution of resources may be along such lines. Lacey in his study of Hightown Grammar (1970) showed that in that school the heads of departments exercised the key roles in the allocation of resources to the students, including the allocation of teachers. Lacey reported that the most senior and experienced teachers tended to be allocated to the upper streams and examination classes. Conversely, 65 per cent of the first and second year teaching and 85 per cent of the bottom stream teaching was done by non-senior or inexperienced teachers. He draws attention to the circular nature of the situation – teachers working with low status classes were usually seen to lack professional standing, and this in turn diminished their capacity to successfully claim materials and equipment for their classes. Such arrangements not only cause a major unevenness in the distribution of resources to different categories of pupil but also leave unanswered more searching questions regarding the appropriate amount of resources each pupil needs or it entitled to.

The incidence of social control may take a less physical form; it may even occur in the classroom of a teacher with a strong commitment to egalitarian reform and social redistribution.

A good example of these difficulties was to be seen in the work of a young teacher in his classroom which the writer was able to see when he undertook a number of periods of observation with his students. The teacher was working in an English primary school, noted for progressive and individualised methods with children ranging from seven through to eleven years of age. The teacher was conducting a project on medical services. For several sessions the classroom became a hospital. The pupils played the roles of doctors, nurses and other hospital personnel. Quite clearly many children were learning not only about anatomy and first aid but also about the diagnosis and decision making central to the work of a hospital service. Yet the writer developed a feeling of unease after this apparently successful project had continued for a number of sessions. Whilst many of the children appeared to be gaining much from the work, a number of others appeared to gain much less.

On inspection children appeared to be divided into three groups. The first was a small group of fluent, confident and generally well spoken children who tended to take the key roles in the project. These children formed the nucleus from which the consultants, matrons, anaesthetists and other key decision makers were regularly drawn. The second rather larger group consisted of children who performed such tasks as nursing assistants, hospital orderlies, porters and a multitude of other 'walk on' parts involving relatively little speech and a minimum of decision making. Most experienced a substantial amount of standing and waiting. The third category not immediately visible were the pool of accident victims. These children spend substantial parts of the sessions on stretchers and swathed in bandages. On occasions these bandages covered not only the limbs but often the face, making speech and even sight and hearing difficult. Not only were these three groups clearly divided in all project activities but also for most part their composition was similar. In many ways this progressive classroom with its strong emphasis on egalitarianism and child-centred approaches showed a remarkable resemblance to the streamed educational arrangements that had preceded it. Though for the teacher all children were 'benefiting' from the rich resources available in this outstandingly well equipped school, some children were unquestionably benefiting more than others. Moreover, the distribution seemed to have a very considerable element of 'social reproduction' built into it.

There are many other examples to be seen in the schools. Ford (1968), in her study of comprehensive schools, showed how in a situation of open access to resources, different categories of children secured a greater share than others. In particular, middle class children seemed to be far more effective at gaining access to the out of school facilities for clubs, sports, drama, hobbies and the like – facilities that in the comprehensive schools under review were often abundantly equipped with appropriate materials and equipment. The process of self-regulated use of resources is often reinforced by the system of cooling out, whereby students come to see themselves as unable or unenthusiastic to follow courses taught by highly qualified, specialist teachers using extensive library and laboratory resources. Instead such pupils 'select' lower status courses. These courses may not necessarily be lower cost ones – metalwork, woodwork and home economics in particular may involve higher material resource cost per student than most other subjects. Yet they are seldom more expensive in their demands on the most costly school resource – that of teachers' salaries.

One of the most developed analyses of social control in the primary school is that of Sharp and Green (1975). The writers show how children may be ascribed identities that appear to make them unsuitable for access to certain kinds of resource in the school. Such a child is Michael:

> Nothing I said would make any difference, you know, he wouldn't ... he didn't want to write or anything, he wasn't very interested in that... He wasn't very interested in joining in with a reading group – he wasn't very interested in the story. He just wanted to go on his own sweet way... he just dribbed and drabbed about ... you know, he never had a true friend. But he's ever so willing to join in if you organise a little group – and he'll join in and he'll be, you know, quite an important member of that group – but he doesn't need to ... I can't make up my mind why he is so peculiar.

Speaking about such children in general one of the teachers at the school under review, 'Mapledene', says:

> In an ideal situation you'd have them all so keen and interested that they'd get on and just come to you for book references and this and that and the other [laughter] but here they don't seem to get involved in anything, not for any length of time anyway. They've got a very short span of concentration, they've got no perseverance at all You've got to be standing over them, all the time, pushing them.

The writers explore in detail the circumstances which lead the teachers to differentiate between children and their resources in this way and to become, despite their evident concern for children, 'agents' of social control. Sharp and Green suggest that this arises from a series of societal expectations that surround the schools and teachers and which are internalised into the personal ideologies of the teachers through the long process of personal and professional socialisation – such a socialisation process inhibits or at least fails to encourage the development of coherent and workable alternative ideologies.

One of the most striking illustrations of the use of resources in the schools is that offered by Wax and Wax (1964) in their account of Indian reservation schoolchildren in North America, an account confirmed by visits of the writer to Canadian reservation schools. They offer a cautionary tale with which to match more superficial analogies of school enrichment strategies. The reservation schools visited by Wax and Wax were abundantly supplied with resources including well qualified teachers and impressive equipment. This favourable allocation arose from a policy of enrichment that attempted to compensate for the deficient educational ecology of the reservations.

On visiting the schools, the researchers found that impressive facilities not only existed but were indeed being put to use. Yet teachers complained that the response of the Indian children was still disappointing, implying in confidence that the whole exercise was a waste of money. The researchers watched several lessons given by white American teachers. One in particular was a lesson on water, dealing with the plumbing systems of a modern American home complete with hot and cold water, drainage and heating systems. The response of the Indian students was minimal despite the impressive efforts of the teacher in presenting his subject with a wide range of teaching aids. The teacher, after the lesson, indicated that this response was, alas, typical. Yet the researchers found that although the understanding of water as used by the white Americans was only faintly grasped by the children they nevertheless had very clear concepts of water that were relevant to their own culture. They were able to speak enthusiastically of mountain streams, fishing, finding water in drought and many other aspects of the theme that had been entirely missing from the lesson they experienced. It is suggested that what is happening in such a situation may be a use of resources by the school in a manner that intensifies feelings of inferiority and even failure on the part of children by demonstrating to them their inadequate knowledge of the 'dominant culture' and the inferiority of their own culture. It may also lead them to accept that the only way that they are likely to be able to obtain high status in American society is to forsake their own culture and begin the long and difficult internalisation of white American culture. Interpretations such as this have led to considerable new debate on the educational resources for Indian schools in both the United States and Canada and attempts to find ways of revaluating the relationship between Indian and white cultures.

Schools and resource take-up

So far our argument has been based on the assumption that, regardless of its ideological orientations, the school distributes its resources fully, and none are wasted. This is not a valid assumption; many local education officers can 'in confidence' name schools where spending on books, materials and equipment is substantially below maximum permitted levels. Heads of schools will speak of wasteful and unnecessary expenditure ceilings. Once again, we are reminded that there is virtually no established attempt to quantify precisely the resources needed by any child for any specific activity. And inevitably there are many inherent areas of 'waste' in any school. An incoming head of department may view the school's existing stock of textbooks in his subject with disdain and insist on their replacement. His reasons for doing so may in part be academic; they may also be in part an attempt to establish the mark of his new regime. New examination regulations or even new editions of texts may lead to the same consequences. The shelves of no longer used textbooks in many school store cupboards testify to the frequency of such changes.

It may also happen that the school rejects or fails to use its resources for other reasons. One of the notable problem areas seems to be connected with major curriculum development projects. Shipman, Bolam and Jenkins (1974), in their study of the Keele Integrated Studies Project, show how, in a number of the trial schools, the extent of resources provided by the project were unused, incompletely used or even misused. The visits to schools suggest that such a state of affairs is in no way uncommon.

A characteristic of curriculum development is the decline of school commitment to a project. Enthusiasm for an innovation is likely to be greatest at the outset. The prospects of a new and 'free' supply of ideas and even resources for the work of the classroom are attractive especially if the project promises to focus resources on some of the more difficult areas of the curriculum where the school is experiencing problems. There is always the prospect that this project will be 'the project', participation in which will bring fame and renown to the school and its teachers.

But as time passes the situation is likely to change. There will inevitably be some problems, possibly many, in the use and adaptation of the project materials to the work of the school. Some successful existing curriculum practices may be challenged and even have to be abandoned if the project is to be taken fully. Timetable changes and other organisational disruptions may be necessary. Key members of staff who are most heavily involved in the project may move to different appointments; this happened frequently in some of the Keele Project schools. In some cases the teacher's very involvement in the project is likely to be the factor in his upward professional mobility. The replacement members of staff may be less interested in the project and certainly will have lacked the initial impetus of the early stages in the school.

Faced with the inevitable difficulties, deprived of the initial leadership in the school and unwilling to abandon successful longstanding practices, marginal staff tend to become more marginal, even disaffected. At the end of the day the usage of many project resources seems to be fragmentary. Some teachers will use a substantial part of the resources provided of the project; most will have adopted bits and pieces and used them to modify, to a greater or lesser extent, their existing resources. Packages will have been taken apart, some of the contents adopted and others discarded. The result will be a melange composed of items from various projects, a range of opinions on how it may be used, further material generated within the school from time to time, the whole gradually modifying the teacher's stock of resources in a highly pragmatic and often unplanned way.

Schools and the creation of resources

The distribution of resources and their acceptance or rejection by the school is of fundamental importance. But the school may also have an active as well as a passive role. in relation to its resources. A number of strategies exist whereby the school creates new demands for resources that local authorities and even the central government may find it difficult not to respond to. A determined school staff can ensure suitable media treatment of the shortcomings of its resources, whether of laboratories or lavatories, that cannot be ignored. In its campaign it may well be supported by professional bodies, parent-teacher associations and local branches of national pressure groups. In times of economic difficulty it may be that successful strategies of this kind provide one of the few certain ways to ensure major advantages in new buildings or special allowances over and above basic 'system maintenance' allocations.

Campaigns do not exhaust the strategies open to schools. An effective way of ensuring new equipment lies within the examination system. If the school is instrumental in introducing a new 'Mode 3' examination syllabus for its students (that is, a syllabus specific to itself) that is subsequently endorsed by the Examination Board, then the local education authority is faced with a *fait accompli*. The necessary materials and equipment to sustain the courses for all the students who follow it are almost certain to be found.

Schools may also be instrumental in introducing new curricula that are endorsed by strong specialist interests such as a local or even a national curriculum development body or even a powerful local employer (a detailed account of some of the ways in which a curriculum project may be established through a school initiative is presented by Eggleston, 1977). Whatever strategy is used, professional or public legitimation of the activity constitutes an important addition to the power of the school to seek official resources to sustain and develop.

Sometimes such initiative may take a very localised form. One example known to the writer occurred in a secondary school serving a large inter-war housing estate. The estate was neglected; the adolescent population had a reputation for vandalism and near delinquency. A small group of newly appointed teachers initiated a

Community Service Project wherein the teachers, with the senior pupils, conducted an impressive programme of socially approved activity whereby the boys and girls dug old people's gardens, painted their walls, cleared the local brook of debris and generally brought acceptable material improvements to a somewhat deprived housing estate. There was widespread local approval for the project and the pupils were praised by the mayor and the local newspaper. There was local relief that the school through its project had 'transformed' the pupils. The local authority voted extra earmarked resources to the school to further the project.

The next phase of the project was based on a realisation that the old people had greater problems than weedy gardens. They had difficulty in obtaining their rate rebates, the local council was tardy in the repair of roofs and other maintenance of a kind that was beyond the scope of the pupils. With the teacher the pupils decided that some further action was needed and wrote to the local newspaper and to the local housing committee about the problems, urging immediate action. The response was quite different in nature from that which they had enjoyed previously. This time the local paper was distinctly unenthusiastic about their 'interference', defining the pupils as 'young troublemakers' and the teachers as 'politically motivated'. The coincidence that the chairman of the Local Housing Committee was also a member of the Local Education Committee appeared to lead to several problems within the school. Certainly the teacher was encouraged not to continue with this particular line of action and the additional resources ceased to be available.

In this 'case study' there is a very obvious and familiar example of the capacity of the school to obtain additional resources either through the local education authority or even from the community at large. And there is also a very clear indication of the way in which the overall process of social control can be imposed upon the work of the school if the school does not appear to be exercising social control through its own initiatives. In this case there was widespread local approval of the adolescents when they appeared to be 'fitting in' more closely to the social system than they had before. This was followed by widespread anxiety when the school appeared to be leading them to participate, however marginally, in local decision making – to exercise some 'power' in the community. Such an initiative by schools opens up the prospect, however minimally, of a redistribution of power in a community, reducing some of the power of those at present exercising it and transferring it to a previously powerless and allegedly 'irresponsible' group. In the example the power sought was in part that which was held by those who also influenced the distribution of educational resources, and the response was predictable. Yet the termination of the project did not mean that it was a failure. The students made visible gains in their capacity to formulate a case, to articulate it effectively and to express it confidently. Several of the students are now playing a part in the power structure of local union branches and one is under consideration for candidature for local government election.

The perception of school resources

The ways resources are interpreted by individuals crucially affect their response to what is provided. The ecology of the school is no exception – it is a different ecology for different individuals. In particular, the perceptions of the children are likely to be fundamentally different from those of the teachers.

On first entering school, the child is likely to be concerned with the spatial aspects of his environment, feeling out the territory available to him in the classroom and in the playground and, particularly, identifying his personal space and its resources – the desks and chairs, the books and pencils, the clothes hooks and aprons. In schools where resources are not compartmentalised and the emphasis is on sharing, it may be that the child has great difficulty in identifying his personal environment. Much the same seems to occur when teachers find that they have to share their. resources – for example, the resources of the day school being also the resources of the evening programme of the community college. Characteristically attempts at compartmentalisation begin with the locked 'evening institute cupboard' standing alongside the locked 'school cupboard', keys being available only to the 'rightful' users. In this way 'they' are prevented from 'abusing' or even wrecking 'our' resources. ...

Unquestionably an important feature of the individual response to the environment of the school is the personal feeling of identity. It may well be that the individual can only use ecological environment in the school and elsewhere if he can make it part of himself by actively relating with it. Nicholson (1972) has gone so far as to suggest in his 'theory of loose parts': that the more successfully designers create a 'no-participant environment' the more successfully will people attempt to participate and establish their individual presence in it, even to the extent of behaviour which is labelled as vandalism. The 'structural modifications' that take place in waiting rooms and public conveniences help to make Nicholson's point, as do the adornments on the books and the carvings on desks in the classroom. It may well be that in our consideration of the provision of the components of the education environment we pay too much attention to their technical qualities and insufficient attention to their personal qualities. There is little doubt that we largely fail to consider the powerful need felt by the individual to personalise his environment – to create a specific and often private ecology rather than a shared one.

Resources and student choice
But the perception of the school's resources is not restricted to their physical properties. Students, teachers, parents and employers characteristically hold perceptions about the nature of school subjects – their usefulness or uselessness, the pleasure or the boredom to which they give rise, their feelings and their relationships towards them. The Schools Council report *Young School Leavers* (1968) shows how strikingly varied such views can be and also how firmly held they commonly are. As the school system takes on a more open and flexible form such views are likely to have increasing consequences for the distribution of resources in schools. In many comprehensive schools and in the greater part of post-school education, course enrolments are predominantly determined by student preference. Though the comprehensive school may provide a wide range of courses for its fourth and fifth year students, if the option course is genuine then some courses are likely to be heavily subscribed and others lightly subscribed, with important consequences not only for the demand for materials and equipment but also for the demand for specialist staffing. Neave (1975) has shown how response to student demand has radically changed the range of course provision in many comprehensive schools in England and Wales,

creating a situation totally different from that of the recent past when heads and senior staff of schools were able to evolve a long term pattern of course provision, secure in the knowledge that they would be able to allocate the 'correct' type and numbers of students to them. It was an era in which the length of school life could be effectively predicted at eleven-plus – those passing the selection examination would almost certainly stay on; those who did not would almost certainly leave at the minimum leaving age. Taylor (1963), in his account of the development of the secondary modern school, charted the persistent efforts of a small band of schools to make resources for extended education available to all who could and wished to use them rather than only to those who had passed the eleven-plus – to help all to 'contract in' to the competitive world of social and educational advancement from which many had been excluded at the eleven-plus. As a consequence of such efforts and the more general changes in the social evaluation of education, students' decisions to stay on are now characteristically made at any time up to minimum leaving age and are, in large measure, made in the light of experience of the resources of the school, particularly the teaching resources, and the personal interpretation of their consequences.

Conclusion

The ecology of the school and the creation, distribution and use of resources that determines it is clearly a partnership between who live and work within it. It is an organic, dynamic environment determined by the multitude of perceptions and intentions of individuals. Yet though characterised by flexibility and at times a remarkably fine balance of forces, the ecology of the school has a remarkable degree of permanence and stability, an underlying form that enables it through many apparently fundamental yet in the long run superficial changes, to continue to take the key role in reproducing the social system from generation. to generation. There is no evidence that individuals seek through their perceptions, their interpretations or their intentions to challenge the ecological system of schooling or of the society of which it is part. Most seem to seek a more active part in the present system rather than in some alternative system – a conclusion that has also been reached after an extensive research in an examination of informal education in England and Wales through

the Youth Service (Eggleston, 1976). It is in the creation and maintenance of this dynamic equilibrium of the schools that the resources
of education play their most crucial and inescapable role.

References

Barnard, G.A., Mc Creath, M., and Freeman, J. (1967) *Notes on the Influence of the
School Curriculum on the Flow of Pupils into Higher Education.* Essex, The
University

Bowles, S. and Gintis, H. (1977) *Schooling in Capitalist America.* London, Routledge

Eggleston, J. (1973) Decision making in the school curriculum. *Sociology* 7.3

Eggleston, J. (1976) *Adolescence and Community.* London, Edward Arnold

Eggleston, J. (1977) *The Sociology of the School Curriculum.* London, Routledge

Ford, J. (1968) *Social Class and the Comprehensive School.* London, Routledge

Lacey, C. (1970) *Hightown Grammar.* Manchester, University Press

Neave, G. (1975) *How They Fared.* London: Routledge

Nicholson, S. (1972) The theory of loose parts. *Studies in Design Education and
Craft,* 4.2

Sharp, R. and Green, A. (1995) *Education and Social Control.* London Routledge

Shipman, M.D., Bowlan, D. and Jenkins, D. (1974) *Inside a Curriculum Project.*
London, Methuen

Steele, F. (1973) *Physical Settings and Organisation Development.* Reading Mass,
Addison Wesley

Vaughan, M. and Archer, M.S. (1971) *Social Conflict and Educational Change in
England and France 1759-1948.* Cambridge, University Press

Wax, M.L. and Wax, R.H. (1964) Formal education in an American Indian community. *Social Problems Monographs* No.2.

7

Work Experience and Schooling

1982, John Eggleston's opening chapter to the
symposium *Work Experience in Secondary Schools*

The relationship between the curriculum and the world of work has always been a challenge, often with a yawning gap between those arguing for a strong early vocational focus and those who wish to keep all aspects of work at arm's length. At the end of the second world war London's schools included nineteen for 'needlework girls' and 24 for 'building boys', with a huge number of ten-year-olds having to choose their adult occupation. In 2002 there was a government-led revival of 'specialist schools'. Yet the curriculum in many secondary schools has hardly brought aspects of occupations into the courses, for instance, of Science or History, Mathematics or English.

John Eggleston brought his sociological studies, his practicality, and his depth of vision of the personal aspects of a school curriculum to a deep and wide-ranging study of the relationship between occupations, ways of life, and adolescent learning. His concern, though, was not that schools should narrowly prepare young people for particular occupations, but that they should relate aspects of work to the education of 'the whole person'. He was a consultant for the OECD project on Adolescence and Work, and Director of the government project on the Educational and Vocational Opportunities of Young People in a Multicultural Society (see Chapter 8). He brought together a wide-ranging and deep exploration of the place of all forms of work experience for adolescents in the symposium of which this was the opening review chapter.

Most subjects have been added to the school curriculum only when informal education by family, church or community becomes unable to ensure the learning needed for adult roles. The history of the '3 Rs', school science, physical education, environmental studies and sex education show that all these subjects have 'arrived' in this way. Vocational education and industrial training became part of the curriculum in areas where pre-occupational training was unavailable informally. Work itself, the newest subject in the curriculum, has a similar history though recent demographic and economic events across the world have speeded the historical process.

In the recent past the experience of work was indivisible from the experience of family, community and society. It is only during the past century and a half that work, for most citizens, has been taken apart from the day-to-day life of family and community and transferred to separate institutions – factories, shops, offices, workshops and warehouses. Such institutions are increasingly 'closed': for reasons of complex technology, security, privacy, hygiene or hazard they are only accessible to those who work therein and within their prescribed working hours.

Yet the twentieth century has seen a further development in the nature of the experience of work. Not only is it a separable part of human experience, but it is also one that is not being made available to all human beings. When twentieth century societies first experienced mass unemployment it was believed that this was but a temporary phenomenon caused by short-term 'malfunctionings' of the economic mechanism such as depression or recession. Now it is realised that unless effective alternative strategies are identified and adopted, such 'malfunctioning' may become a permanent feature: unemployment become structural.

Young people and work

In this new situation major problems arise for young people. By far the majority are beyond the reach of any school 'remedy' and it is misleading and dangerous to imply otherwise. But some have considerable relevance for the work of schools. One is that in many countries unemployment, especially for the young, co-exists with unfilled vacancies in many of the areas of work which require skills, understandings and attributes not generally possessed by school leavers. Thus there are shortages of young people for vacancies in the 'servicing trades' responsible for the maintenance of motor cars, television sets and other domestic appliances, building maintenance and even gardening and window cleaning. There are also recurring shortages of candidates for higher level work in computing, electronics and a range of scientific and creative occupations. Of course, not all of these shortages are 'real', some are 'technical', but there is little doubt that many do exist.

A second problem is that young people who leave school and do not experience work seem to find it increasingly difficult to obtain it. Potential employers believe that some kind of atrophy develops; just as the muscles in a broken leg lose their power, so a total lack of work experience is believed to diminish the capacity to satisfy the very requirements of work such as industry, responsibility and punctuality.

A third, and perhaps the most fundamental, problem is closely associated with the second; it is that work experience provides the basic contexts for 'normal' life. These include the use of time, the achievement of social 'standing' with its rights and duties and many of the attitudes and values that underpin participation in all the other human contexts offered by society. We may express the situation in two ways. One is that vocational identity is the key to social identity. The other is that work is the central instrument of social control in modern societies. Without the experience of work, how can the individual develop an adequate social identity and how can the society exercise the social control over its members necessary to achieve stability and continuity?

The experience of work

We have now come to the crucial nature of work experience. Like most human experiences, it has been taken for granted while its existence seemed assured. We have come to see its importance more clearly when its availability is at risk. It is necessary to notice, however, that work experience involves a dual context. One is the context of the specific job being done – with its skills, expectations, norms and values. The other is the context of the labour market with its organisations of labour and management, its norms of production, payment and security. Both aspects will be examined in the consideration of work experience provided by the schools.

Almost all young people see work as the key to the achievement of full masculinity or femininity. Willis's study of working-class boys in an English comprehensive school in an inner-city area depicts the social pressures on the boys to take their place on the shop floor and so earn the acceptance of the community to which they belong (1978). These boys need to prove themselves amongst their workmates as capable of facing and surviving the realities of the factory floor with its 'hard and brutalising' conditions.

Willis writes:

> The lads are not choosing careers or particular jobs, they are committing themselves to a future of generalised labour. Most work – or the 'grafting' they accept they will face – is equilibrated by the overwhelming need for instant money, the assumption that all work is unpleasant and that what really matters is the potential particular work situations hold for self and particularly masculine expression, diversions and 'laffs' as learnt creatively in the counter-school culture. These things are quite separate from the intrinsic nature of any task. This view does not contradict, for the moment, the overwhelming feeling that work is something to look forward to ... the lure of the prospect of money and cultural membership amongst 'real men' beckons very seductively as refracted through their own culture.

But as the lads' attitudes clearly show, of even greater importance than specific occupational role is the set of understandings and the self-image that the individual brings to his roles. This identity with which the individual imbues his roles is crucial to the way he plays them, modifies them and develops them, and to his own personal future within them. A label, such as lathe operator, is but an incomplete guide to human behaviour in work – the identity with which the incumbent fills the role is the key component. How does he perceive himself as a lathe operator? He has chosen the work or is it a forced decision? If the former, what are his alternatives? Are they realistic or only based on fantasy? How does he adjust to the role in the absence of alternatives? What are the implications for his other social behaviour? Fundamentally, is the vocational identity, with all its consequences, compatible with his ego and his self-image? If it is not, how may greater compatibility develop within the role?

The development of vocational identities is complex in modern society. In early, labour-intensive industrialisation, when large numbers of workers were required to perform routine and repetitive tasks, individual identity seldom came to exercise a dominant influence on production. Their self-image was of relatively little consequence to most employers. Young people were fitted into their roles in conditions which Durkheim described as 'mechanical solidarity'; the role transcendent, the individual subordinate.

The concept of identity alerts us to an alternative process. It is one in which young people may prefer to 'contract in' to both the specific job and the labour market generally rather than to accept them passively. This new approach is highly relevant to some aspects of contemporary social conditions. It is compatible with the expressed views of young people who wish to 'count for something' in society rather than to be 'on the receiving end' of 'the system'. But it is also appropriate for the needs of some sectors of modern industry which calls for human beings not to act as 'machines', but to use their capacity to adapt, adjust and initiate. For such occupational roles an active vocational identity rather than a passive vocational role is highly preferable.

Unless an acceptable vocational identity can be achieved, then life for the individual is likely to be at best incomplete or compartmentalised; at worst, frustrating, enervating and incompatible. Problems are likely to arise not only for the individual, but also for society – which is likely to experience widespread alienation or disruptive behaviour if vocational identities are generally felt to be unsatisfactory. And if work is not available the problems are likely to occur in an even more serious form.

The achievement of work identity

We have already noted that, until recently, most vocational identities were acquired by predominantly informal means. The learning of occupational roles literally began in the cradle as the child saw his parents at work in homes, farms and workshops. The phrase 'like father like son' epitomised not only the informality of learning but also the predictability of the vocational role that awaited most young people. The circumstances of the parents determined the future role of the young and the learning appropriate to it. Such identities were strongly reinforced by the norms of the community which defined, often with great precision, such things as man's work and woman's work; noble work and base work. Definitions of this kind were sometimes strongly reinforced by initiation ceremonies as a prelude to entry to adult vocational roles and still feature in some apprentice-ship schemes.

Informal mechanisms for achieving vocational identities are, how-ever, not always appropriate in modern dynamic societies, where occupational structures are changing rapidly and in which it may be possible for young people to have sufficient knowledge of the available roles in sufficient time to learn them and identify with them in anticipation. A characteristic problem of all advanced indus-trial societies is the rapid growth of new occupational groups such as electronics engineers, motor car repairers and salesmen, advertis-ing and sales personnel, which has meant that many young people enter work to undertake roles for which they have been able to achieve little or no preliminary identification. New generations of vocational identity may commence with each new initiative in tech-nology and commerce.

School and vocational identity

Schools have usually played only a small part in helping young people to achieve vocational identity. Though in the past half-cen-tury they have come to exercise a major role in helping to identify talent through the examination and accreditation systems, there has been little attempt to assist the young in achieving the identities to accompany the examination qualifications. There has been even less success in helping those without examination qualifications to achieve such identities. This has led to many problems. Not only have many young people lacked an adequate identity for work but also, for many, for the other aspects of life that are linked to work. There has, for example, been remarkably little preparation for such activities as leadership in the workers' unions – roles that undeniably play a central part in modern societies. As a result, there are major problems in identifying leaders for these bodies at both local and regional level with important consequences for the day-to-day running of our occupational and economic systems. Political and community identities also have seldom received the attention they deserve; potential leaders here too are often in short supply.

An important element in vocational identity has commonly been the social background of the young. Many writers have drawn attention to the small part played by schools in orienting and preparing young people for work. Becker (1963) has suggested that school makes little impact other than to offer legitimation of the differences brought about by home and community. As Willis (1978) says: 'The difficult thing to explain about how middle class kids get middle class jobs is why others let them. The difficult thing to explain about how working class kids get working class jobs is why they let themselves.'

Bourdieu (1972) sees this to be a consequence of dominance of social and cultural reproduction processes that schools reinforce but do not change. Many writers, such as Lazerson (1971) and Bowles and Gintis (1976), have come to see the growing potential importance of school as a transition institution into the labour force; an institution which 'accredits' young people with the various needs of the labour market (including unemployment) and achieves the necessary correspondence between supply and demand. Grubb and Lazerson (1981) demonstrate ways in which even new strategies of career education have, in practice, been used to stratify the school system, and to separate lower-class and ethnic minority youth from their white and middle-class peers.

Providing work experience in the schools

Yet despite the difficulties, the present-day economic and social systems compel schools to take an active role in the achievement of work identity and the provision of experience in which it may occur. Watts (1981) writes:

> The world of work is central to our society, and to the generation and distribution of wealth within it. For schools to neglect the world of work behind rhetoric like 'concern for the whole person' – as though the role of worker was not an important *part* of the whole person – is abjectly to neglect a critical part of their educational responsibilities....
> The need for schools to address the world of work, but to do so in a

critical and dynamic way, is all the more important because of the crisis that is taking place in relation to the place of work in our society.

The new planned work experience schemes in schools take many forms. Essentially, they are interventionist strategies designed to provide a substitute experience of work when the 'normal' social forces fail to deliver 'the real thing'. Work experience is, of course, a long way from the real thing: it can offer work tasks in work environments, but it cannot offer normal pay and tenure – essential adjuncts to identity as a worker.

There have always been some educators who have believed that work experience is too important to leave to chance – or just to be talked about in the schools. J.S Mill, J. Dewey and Kurt Hahn advocated this view strongly and in different ways it is embodied in the curricula of the German Technical High Schools and the Soviet Young Pioneers. But in present conditions, when work experience cannot be relied upon 'just to happen' for the majority of young people, its provision becomes an urgent social need. In some countries it has become a major focus of national politics. Australia provides a typical example. In November 1979 the Commonwealth and States announced a series of initiatives known as the School-to-Work Transition Programme. $259 million are being spent over the next five years on a range of technical courses, student counselling and special programmes for young people. The reason for the government's action was obvious. Already one young Australian in five was out of work, and another 50,000 were due to enter the labour market with little or no hope of a job.

In Australia – as in the United States, Denmark, Britain and almost every other developed country – inevitably the issues are polarised in political debate. On the one hand, there is enthusiasm for 'educational solutions' – to offer the opportunity for the young to acquire more fully the skill, knowledge, attitudes and perceptions along with as much as possible of the experience needed to constitute a vocational identity. On the other hand, there is the view that creation of more jobs is the only worthwhile objective; if this is done adequately the rest can once again be left to chance. The contributors to this volume are largely, but not solely, concerned with examining the former position. At its fullest considerations the latter, involving changes in the total structure of societies, often of a radical nature, is beyond the scope of the schools. But it may be argued that many of the 'educational' solutions, far from being palliative, have the capacity to create jobs within existing societies and a number of schools are already involved in putting this capacity into practice.

Variations between practice in schools are widespread as befits a developing field. The categorisation of process is presented in some detail in the forthcoming pages. The categories used are:

> Infusion
> Work experience courses
> Work creation schemes
> Link courses
> Work simulation schemes.

Infusion

We may begin with one of the oldest forms of work experience – that in which it is *infused* into the total curriculum rather than constituting a separate *additional* activity. Only recently has this total approach been labelled as infusion – a term now widely used in the United States. Yet for centuries schools have provided work experience exactly relevant for the needs of their elite students – those who are entering the learned and academic professions. Such students have experienced working in the academic library, acting as teachers with titles such as monitor or prefect, conducting religious worship, and much else. Alas, such work experience has offered little to those who were not destined for academic, clerical, legal or library careers: schools have often been castigated for their concern for the future work of the few rather than the many. More recently, however, a conscious strategy of infusion has brought work experience into the whole curriculum for some students. Science has concerned itself with the practice of science in industry, mathematics with its commercial and business utilisation, linguistics with careers in communication at all levels. In particular, work in design, craft and technology has been closely linked with the experience of industrial production – indeed the subject area has gone under the title of Industrial Arts in many countries. In all these activities, visits to industry and from industrialists form an important feature. The argument for such infusions is that preparation for work is not just another subject – it is what school is all about.

Though compellingly straightforward in principle, the practice of infusion is difficult. Quite apart from the problems of examinations, even when coherently planned as in the Schools Council Industry Project, the generations of tradition and academic teacher selection and training make it difficult for both schools and teachers to make the radical change across the board, whilst its very diffusion makes it difficult to evaluate. The objectives are easy to list, the achievements are distinctly harder to identify. Perhaps the way forward is to develop work experience as a well-established activity of the school system first and then to integrate it effectively in the whole curriculum. Certainly, the 'additive' arrangements which we now go on to describe seem, in the short run at least, to be able to offer more identifiable results.

Work experience courses

These are perhaps one of the best established of the 'additive' solutions within the schools. In such courses older pupils visit one or more vocational locations where they have the opportunity, over a period, to mix with workers at a variety of levels and to learn something of the formal and the informal culture of the work-place – the ways in which life is experienced by those who work therein. In some situations it is possible for pupils actually to experience work with its productive rhythms, its rewards and constraints, but unfortunately problems of union restrictions, insurance hazard and many other administrative difficulties generally restrict such opportunities to casual work and certain kinds of agricultural situations. (Though in England and Wales some enabling legislation exists – such as the Education Work Experience Act of 1973.) Such courses are well-known, although some variations – such as 'shadowing' (where a pupil shadows an adult throughout his working day) – are less familiar. They fit happily into the contemporary orientation of many secondary schools where renewed emphases are being placed upon initiation into the life of the community. Such emphases have followed a recognition in that although children spend most of their life outside the school, they none the less have surprisingly few *entrees* into the adult world that exists beyond their homes and in the immediate neighbourhood. Whereas in the past, children encountered working adults in many contexts and had many opportunities to identify with them, they may now seldom see a working adult other than the postman and the dustman. Work experience courses attempt to fill this dearth of first-hand experience.

The aims of work experience courses are well stated in the Department of Education and Science (England and Wales) *Circular 7/74* of 1974. It states:

> The principle which should underlie any work experience scheme is that pupils should be given an insight into the world of work, its disciplines and relationships. This principle, and the requirement of the Act that schemes for pupils of compulsory school age must form part of an educational programme, would not be satisfied by arrangements made whether in school or elsewhere, whose purpose was specifically or mainly to assess individuals for particular forms of employment, or to occupy pupils in producing articles for sale.

There are numerous examples of well-developed work experience courses in secondary schools. Many schools have made such sophisticated and successful arrangements with local industry and provide placements of varying durations. Some, but by no means all, are undertaken in connection with the Schools Council Industry Project.

Many schools report a range of favourable outcomes from their work experience courses. A recurring one is that such courses establish links between industries and schools that did not exist before and that work opportunities previously unknown to the school become available to its pupils as a result. In some cases pupils are offered employment well before the completion of the course. There may, of course, be problems – a highly popular work experience course in a school may siphon off some of the pupils selected by the school for advanced courses in polytechnics or universities. For these and many other reasons, it is widely seen to be desirable to accompany work experience with appropriate guidance; the arrangement whereby guidance counsellors are linked to the pre-employment courses in the Irish schools is a good example of such strategies.

A typical example of work experience at various levels is that provided by the Swiss in most cantons. There work experience involves three stages (which may not exist in all schools and cantons):

1   visits to enterprises – usually of a few hours' duration to sample the ambience of the work place;

2   following student responses, extended conversations about work in the workplace with experienced workers;

3   extended experiences in the workshop of 3-6 days.

This last is a relatively new scheme called *Schnupperlehre*, literally a 'sniff of learning' and is already available in the Cantons of Berne and Zurich. It appears likely to be adopted more widely in the near future. Notwithstanding their traditional appearance, these arrangements have a new and important role to play in Swiss affairs. Until recently, foreign guest-workers have performed most of the low status, 'dirty' jobs, allowing most Swiss to do higher status work. Since the economic recession, many guest-workers have been 'sent home', and their work is now being done by Swiss. A crucial task of the schools and guidance services is to make such work more 'acceptable' to the young; the *Schnupperlehre* plays an important role in this. A further emergent role of the *Schnupperlehre* appears to be to provide an opportunity for employers to select prospective employees; in addition to giving the young 'a sniff of work' it gives the employers a sniff of the young. One of the consequences of such a scheme is, inevitably, that it offers participants an early start in job-selection, which may thereby disadvantage non-participants.

Work creation schemes

Closely linked with the provision of work experience – and a logical extension from it – is the creation or identification of work not currently being undertaken by existing paid labour. Here the school is not only able to provide work experience, but also to provide necessary services for the community. The report of the CERES project in Brunswick, Melbourne describes an urban environment field station project involving the reconstitution of ten acres of degraded urban land with community gardens, city farm, environmental displays, low energy building, low energy display and a community meeting place for community use and community support, public environmental education and training, school and tertiary projects, energy research and development, educational recreation and developing employment opportunities. The genesis of the project lay in the liaison of the seven local secondary schools in a joint. body, the Brunswick Secondary Education Council (BRUSEC) and its work with a range of statutory and voluntary bodies. A detailed record of the project is available (Coles, 1979).

Work creation schemes such as these can only make a small contribution to the availability of jobs; they cannot transform the economic system and are open to many criticisms. One is that they generate 'slave labour'; another is that they focus on low-level skill. Yet a third is that when all schools offer such schemes the oversupply will be so great as to be self-defeating. But in the early stages, at least, work creating schemes seem effective and it would be folly to anticipate or overreact to the criticisms.

Link courses

A less well-known form of school programme is that of the link course. In such courses, senior school pupils spend part of their time out of school in the community and vocational colleges and factory schools which are attended by young people already at work. Here the opportunity to work alongside workers and to learn and understand their views is seen to have many advantages, even though it is taking place within a college rather than a work situation. Skinner (1970), Principal of Melton Mowbray College of Further Education, England, writing about such a link course based in his college, comments:

> By a 'Link. Course' I mean, not isolated visits to a college, or a purely college organised class, but a fully integrated course between school and college, involving a truly joint approach, whereby the staffs of both institutions not only co-operate together in their approach, but are seen by the students consciously to do so, in such a way that each teacher is capitalising on the work of the other within an integrated whole.

Work simulation schemes

Yet another form of programme is the work simulation scheme. Such schemes involve the creation of work situation in school. For example, school workshops may be used to set up a production line system in which a basic object – a Christmas card, a coat hook or a toy may be 'mass produced' and in which all aspects of production – product design, market research, trial production, quantity production, quality control, marketing, accounting and much else, may be incorporated. A wide range of experience can be concentrated in well-designed schemes, and many of the determinants of modern vocational identities – the economies of scale, the concept of labour intensity, cost-benefit analyses, and so on, can be incorporated. Such understandings are all too commonly incompletely held by many working adults – even at senior levels.

Douglas (1975) investigated a number of these projects and reports:

> The investigation found that school-based factory projects embraced a wide area of activity, ability and experience, involving greater scope than had, at first, been anticipated. For example, two mixed secondary schools in Lincolnshire undertook experimental programmes involving production line projects and demonstrated that the approach was feasible for both boys and girls, while in North Wales a low ability school leavers' class in one school became motivated and industrious for the first time when given the opportunity to produce articles as a viable commercial undertaking.

The characteristics of school work experience programmes

All the forms of school programme have three aims in common. The first is to increase the possibility of employment and to ensure a more effective linkage between the role of the student and the role of the worker and to facilitate the transition between school and work so that dissonance and disturbance to the young person, his fellow workers, his employers, his family and his community is reduced.

The second feature of all such projects is that they embody a knowledge content. All identify a body of understandings, skills, values and orientations which, it is believed, are valuable components of vocational identity. All too often, however, this knowledge content is largely determined, if not wholly so, by the adult participants. Yet we are increasingly aware that the understandings of the young people themselves provide a crucial component of their vocational identity and that, unless they are taken into account in devising such programmes, it is likely that the achievement will fall far short of what might have been possible. The incomplete recognition of the highly important understandings of young people is clearly to be seen in the quotation from Willis's work that has already been used. It is also portrayed by Webb in his account of Black School (1962):

> What sort of person would the boy become who accepted the standards the teacher tries to impose? In himself he would be neat, orderly, polite and servile. With the arithmetic and English he absorbed at school, and after further training, he might become a meticulous clerk, sustained by a routine laid down by someone else, and piously accepting his station in life. Or, if he got a trade, we can see him later in life clutching a well-scrubbed lunch tin and resentful at having to pay union dues, because the boss, being a gentleman, knows best. To grow up like this a lad has to be really cut-off from the pull of social class and gang, which luckily few of the boys at Black School are, because both these types are becoming more and more redundant as mechanisation increases and job content decreases.

Yet a third issue of school-based schemes is the range of adult participants. Unquestionably, teachers must play an important, if not the central, part in their organisation. Teachers who have previous experience in adult occupations other than teaching are likely to have a particularly valuable contribution to make (though much depends on the perceptions of work held by such teachers). But in addition to teachers, it is important that adults, who are themselves working in industry, participate: it is even more important that these include people who are doing the jobs to which pupils are immediately aspiring. Only in this way is effective and acceptable communication likely to be achieved.

The evaluation of work experience

How may one evaluate the context of school-based work experience? How can we tell if the visit to the factory is no more significant to the lives of the young than a visit to see the lions at the zoo?

We shall leave aside the consequences for administrations and institutions who find work experience schemes invaluable for maintaining high participation rates or even because they can be used to demonstrate that they are 'doing something' to solve a problem. But an evaluation of the consequences for young people is considerably harder to achieve. Overall, young people seem to enjoy work experience schemes; evidence in most available reports suggests that they are seen to be interesting and certainly less boring than other aspects of school. Attendance during work experience programmes often runs at a consistently higher level than participation in 'normal' school.

Beyond this the evidence is ambiguous. There is some evidence that work experience is related to a better chance of obtaining jobs in cognate occupations – figures of 60-70 per cent are quoted for some parts of the Swiss *Schnupperlehre* project and some of the Australian schemes. But this placement effect may only be at the expense of those who do not participate in work experience schemes – in fact, a displacement effect! Similar uncertainty occurs where extensive post-school work experience schemes are financed by governments – are the young people on work experience used to do work that is otherwise done by 'normal' workers who are then made redundant; in other words, does work experience reduce the number of available jobs? Evidence here can be no more than suggestive.

The vocational identity consequences too are unsure. Whilst work experience may reinforce vocational and workskills in a specific occupation, it may reduce the choice of the individual by inducing 'premature specificity' and run counter to a broader careers education or counselling programme. The increasing dominance of work experience programmes in the lives of young people could well lead to a decline in their acceptance of apparently 'less relevant' aspects of their educational experience. Indeed, the very acceptability of work experience programmes may diminish the overall acceptability of the school. Such realisations account for a good deal of the criticisms of the programmes made by 'regular academic' teachers in the schools, other reasons being the belief of such teachers that work experience schemes divert funds from regular programmes and bring in 'deviant, lefty' teachers with disruptive consequences. Such teachers are likely to be dismayed by a suggestion from Sweden that when three days a week are devoted to work experience and two days to schooling the school achievement remains equal to that of five days' schooling.

This is, of course, not to suggest that the young find all aspects of work experience programmes attractive. Writers such as Ryrie and Weir (1978) show that such programmes can not only accelerate positive work identities but also lead to negative ones and even alienation. Such evaluations reaffirm the need for programmes to be linked with guidance and follow-up schemes: indeed, such a linkage constitutes one of their most significant prospective advantages, though one that is seldom realised fully.

One of the more evident features of all work experience schemes is to emphasise the instrumental rather than the expressive aspects of schooling. Goals such as serving the needs of the economy, helping young people to contribute to society and even 'strengthening law and order' are not uncommonly linked with the practice of work experience. There is some evidence that many students respond to this instrumental approach as in Monk's study of pupils' identities (1981). Yet this instrumentalism stands in sharp contrast to many of the experience goals espoused by teachers and youth and community workers in recent decades as Davies (1981) has demonstrated.

A recurring evaluation of work experience courses arises from the position of their participants in the social system. Gleeson and Mardle (1980) and many other writers notice that there are three 'strands' of young people – those who proceed direct from school to university, college or professional training, those who proceed direct to work or work and training 'on the job' and those who have difficulty in obtaining work at all. Even many schools' work experience schemes are predominantly followed by the 'bottom third', those in the upper band and even in the middle band tend to regard it as a frill – a view often shared by their parents.

This brings us to one of the most important series of criticisms of work experience schemes, that they are no more than a re-styled and updated version of the vocational education programme of the early years of the present century. Though a product of the progressive era of American education, such programmes came to be seen by many as no more than placebos to accompany the process of fitting working-class children into working-class jobs, 'a second-class education in the interest of class stratification' (Grubb and Lazerson, 1981). These authors mount a trenchant critique of vocationalism in education in all its forms:

> the goals of vocational education are clear enough – and they are distinctly different from the view that education should develop every aspect of human potential, including the critical facilities and capabili-

ties for self-motivated activity. That vision of education, associated particularly with John Dewey, has often been suspected of creating dissatisfied, unruly workers who are disrespectful of authority, and of encouraging educational 'frills' like art and music. In contrast, during those periods when the schools have threatened to become 'useless', vocationalism has been ready to reassert that all of schooling should be evaluated by its contributors to the economic system – and to an economic system that itself is beyond criticism.

No amount of training, and especially no amount of skill-specific training, can make teenagers eligible for jobs which require some higher education; and training programmes cannot reverse the growth of secondary labour market jobs which provide some employment for teenagers but induce them to be unsatisfied and unstable workers. To the extent that credentialing is responsible for youth unemployment, then, training programmes cannot resolve the problem.

It is certainly true that school-based programmes can do little to overcome this structural condition of the labour markets for young people, as all critics recognise. Yet to accept such a negative viewpoint as being sufficient would return schools to the passive position many felt obliged to adopt in the early 1970s when, following Jencks (1972), it was widely asserted that 'schools make no difference'. A decade later many researches show the fallacy of this assertion – though the differences made by schooling are far less dramatic and rapid than those anticipated in the 1960s.

The same small but often significant consequences are regularly being identified in the evaluation of work experience programmes. Thus Arai's (1980) report on forty-six experimental high schools identified by the Italian Ministry of Education reported that only nine were aiming at work experience as part of the regular curriculum. He concludes:

> The slightly disappointing results of these ambitious programmes are understandable in view of the meagre material and human resources devoted to the project and of the poor state of preparedness on the part of both schools and teachers. The key to success lies, however, not in improvements of these conditions but in making teachers concerned realise that work experience programmes constitute a central rather than a peripheric part of high school education.

This finding links with those of Farrar (1978) in her studies at the Huron Institute, USA, which show that one of the key features in the success of programmes (however evaluated) lies in the degree of commitment of the participants, not only teachers and students, but also employers.

Farrar, in her summing up, suggests that some of the strongest features of work experience programmes lie in their capacity to stimulate and motivate young people and thereby enhance schooling and its effectiveness. Yet she notes that it is precisely the other 'political' justifications – job experience, improved employment prospects that are usually argued – the very justifications that have been found to be unprovable at best, questionable at worst.

Some of the most important aspects of evaluation are also the most difficult. In two interesting but as yet unpublished studies of the self-image of unemployed youth, Gurney (1980 a and b) dispels the simplistic view that unemployment is lowering to the self-image. Rather, it is that getting a job is a route to enhanced self-esteem, especially for the girls. She writes: 'Prior to leaving school, girls had significantly lower self-esteem than boys. Those girls who found employment soon after leaving school showed a significant increase in self-evaluation, but no change was found in the level of self-esteem for males or the unemployed of either sex.'

Hebling (1979), in a study of vocational maturity, self-concepts and identity, obtained results that readily link with those of Gurney. Though more specifically focused to higher education, they are worth quoting here:

> Vocational maturity is clearly, although not strongly, correlated with two different factors: work adjustment and a sense of personal identity (self-esteem is included in the latter). It seemed useful to make a distinction between central and peripheral aspects of vocational maturity ... It may be concluded from our data that vocationally mature students who run the risk of becoming problem cases in higher education, are mostly to be found among those who are not work oriented, have low self confidence and low self-esteem, and do not have a strong sense of identity or have problems with their personal identity.

A number of studies of the development of adolescent identity emphasise that much of the development occurs as a consequence of the establishment of a differentiation from schooling and that work experience, perceived as part of schooling, is no exception. Such studies question the advantage of making work experience too integrated a component of schooling as, for many adolescents, the need to differentiate themselves from the experience would be counter-productive.

The evaluation of the clients

There is a great deal of informal evaluation by the young people themselves. Very much of it is unfavourable: 'You know all that work experience at school – well it's just a waste of time.' 'A right send-up that school visit to the brick works – my mates there were splitting their sides at the things they told the teachers.' Yet there is plenty of evidence that more perceptive appraisals of young people exist that display an acute awareness of the benefits as well as the problems of work experience programmes.

Gleeson and Mardle (1980) report Andy's views which illustrate a considerable capacity to discriminate between projects.

> I wouldn't get the same opportunities off a craft course would 1? ... Craft work is too limited ... there aren't enough opportunities to do really skilled work. Nowadays, most craft jobs are boring...repetitive work on machinery ... where you don't use your brain. 1 wouldn't do a craft course ... if you do, you're stuck . . . you haven't got the same chances or choices, have you? You've only got to look around this place .... Most of the craft lads aren't interested in their work or college ... they didn't do so well at school to get on to a technician's course ... they're stuck ... they haven't got a future outside craft work. If I couldn't get a job as a technician ... or something like it ... 1 certainly wouldn't take craft work.

It is also evident that a very great deal of the learning of young people consists of the reaffirmations of established beliefs about the nature of work. Delamont (1980), in a study of adolescent girls, notices the way in which girls' expectations of sex differentiation in work is powerfully reinforced by their experiences of both work and school. Far from such experiences leading a girl to enter a 'non-feminine' occupation like engineering, they appear more likely to deter her.

Many of the individual teachers also offer sensitive evaluations. Watts (1980) summarises some of the available evaluatory evidence:

> Overall, it would seem from the available evidence that the vocational, anticipatory and placing effects are more valued by young people than the social-educational effects emphasised by the policymakers. Of these, the placing effects are the most suspect, because any advantage acquired is to a large extent acquired at the expense of other groups in the labour market. In this respect work experience is merely what Hirsch (1977) called a 'positional good': if it were extended to all, its benefits would disappear. In policy terms, therefore, its case has to be argued in terms not of the benefits it bestows on its participants, but of the net social benefit once negative effects on those who suffer are taken into account. A case could be argued here for positive discrimination in favour of young people entering the labour market to enable them to compete with those already in it. An argument along these lines was offered by a Project Trident co-ordinator:

> One thing that's been said to me several times by employers is something to the effect that they didn't know schools still turned out youngsters of the quality of the one they just had.

Such evaluations, loose, imprecise and elusive as they are, are the best guide we have to the achievements of work experience. In this area of education, more than in any other, it is the client's experience and appraisal of these programmes and the opportunity, legitimation and accreditation they offer him which will ultimately determine the size, nature and direction of future provision. In so doing, they will largely determine whether programmes built in and after school will mark the beginning of a new relationship of education and work in modern societies, possibly involving some aspects of a 'youth guarantee' or merely involve an acceptance of the existing structure often offering only palliatives to non-achievers.

Our understandings remain incomplete; Musgrave (1980) makes the central point well in an unpublished paper:

> My thesis is that we must stop seeing the link between school and work as the focal relationship. The link is working not perfectly nothing ever does in a free society, but at least reasonably well and many existing social forces will force improvement where deficiencies exist. We must begin to redefine work and relate our view of work and of leisure to education so that we can evolve some policy that is appropriate to

the probable economic circumstances at the start of the second millennium, a date when those leaving school at the end of this year will still be only thirty-five. But above all we must initiate the discussions that make possible the political decisions that will ensure commitment to a new social reality, which as always we ourselves shall in large part create.

What Musgrave is arguing for is a re-examination of 'life experience' to accompany the changes that we have been examining in work experience, To undertake such a re-examination is an even more difficult task than to examine curriculum, work experience or guidance as separate items... These experiences can and should become a dominant part of the curriculum. No longer should work experience be left to chance occurrence in life after school or contrived by other agencies.

References

Arai, P. (1980) 'Modern Society and Work Experience Programmes in Schools', *Secondary Education*, February.

Baker, C. (1978) 'Becoming Adolescent: The Shaping of Identity in the Junior Secondary Years', paper presented at SAANZ Conference, Brisbane, Australia.

Ball, C., and Ball, M. (1979), *Fit for Work?* London, Writers and Readers Publishing Co-operative.

Becker H. (1963) *Outsiders: Studies in the Sociology of Deviance*, New York, Free Press.

Bourdieu, P. (1972) 'Cultural Reproduction and Social Reproduction', in R. Brown (ed.), *Knowledge, Education and Cultural Change*, London, Tavistock.

Bowles, S., and Gintis, H. (1976) *Schooling in Capitalist America*, London: Routledge and Kegan Paul.

Coles, P. (1979) *The CERES Project*, Victoria, Australia, The Brunswick Secondary Education Council.

Coles, P. (1980) *Report of the Victoria Employment Committee Working Party on Work Experience*, Victoria, Australia, Victorian Employment Committee.

Davies, B. (1981) 'Beyond the work ethic', *Times Educational Supplement*, Friday, 13 November 1981.

Delamont, S. (1980) *Sex Roles and the School*, London, Methuen.

Douglas, M.H. (1975) 'Industrial Design and Production Projects in Secondary Schools', *Studies in Design Education and Craft*, 8. 1.

Farrar, S. (1978) 'The Evaluation of Work Programmes', Huron, The Institute, mimeo.

Gleeson, D., and Mardle, G.D. (1980) *Further Education or Training? A Case Study in the Theory and Practice of Day-Release Education*, London, Routledge and Kegan Paul.

Grubb, W.N., and Lazerson, M. (1981) 'Vocational Solution to Youth Problems: the Persistent Frustrations of the American Experience', *Educational Analysis*, 3, 2, pp. 91-104.

Gurney, R.M. (1980a) 'Aspects of School Leaver Unemployment', University of Melbourne, mimeo.

Gurney, R.M. (1980b) 'Does Unemployment Affect the Self Esteem of School Leavers?', University of Melbourne, mimeo.

Hebling, H. (1979) *Vocational Maturity, Self-Concepts and Identity,* Paris, OECD.

Hirsch, F. (1977) *Social Limits to Growth*, London, Routledge and Kegan Paul.

Ivison, V. (1979) 'Young Enterprise – a school industry link', Trends H.

Jamieson, L, and Lightfoot, M. (1981) 'Learning About Work', *Educational Analysis*, 3.2.

Jencks, C. (1972) *Inequality: a Reassessment of the Effect of Family and Schooling in America*, London, Allen Lane.

Lazerson, M. (1971) *Origins of the Urban School*, Cambridge, Mass., Harvard University Press.

Monk, M.J. (1981) 'The Classroom Nexus', unpublished PhD thesis, University of London.

Musgrave, P.W (1980) 'Contemporary Schooling, Competence and Commitment to Work', Monash University, mimeo.

Ryrie, A.C., and Weir, A.D. (1978) *Getting a Trade*, London, Hodder and Stoughton (for the Scottish Council for Research in Education).

Skinner, W.G. (1970) 'Link Courses in Colleges of Further Education' Part I, *Survey 4*, Staffordshire, Keele University (for Schools Council), April.

Watts, A.G. (1980) 'Work Experience Programmes – the views of British Youth', Paris, OECD, mimeo.

Watts, A.G. (1981) 'Schools Work and Youth: An Introduction', *Educational Analysis*, 3.2, pp. 1-6.

Webb, J. (1962) 'The Sociology of a School', *British Journal of Sociology*, vol. XIII, no. 3.

Willis, P. (1978) *Learning to Labour*, London, Saxon House.

8

Education for Some

Education for Some: the Educational and Vocational Experiences
of 15-18 year-old Members of Minority Ethnic Groups *by John
Eggleston, David Dunn and Madhu Anjali. Trentham 1986*

*When it was commissioned by the Department of Education and
Science, the research led by Professor Eggleston into the educational
and vocational experiences of black 15-18 year olds was to be an
adjunct to research into 'the underachievement of West Indian children in our schools'. This they duly published in 1985 as the Swann
report,* Education for All. *But the government never published the
Eggleston report (as intended) and for almost a year it was only
available in photocopied form, from Keele University, at great expense and bulk. The report did not endear John to the DES, which
published two heavy tomes on the new mathematics curriculum on
the same day as the report was released, prompting the education
correspondent of the* Telegraph *to ask John whether the government
was 'trying to bury' it.*

In 1986, Education for Some: the Educational and Vocational Experiences of 15-18 year-old Members of Minority Ethnic Groups
*was edited from the Keele University Report and published by the
fast-growing Trentham Books that John had co-founded, under the
title* Education for Some.

*It pointed up the racial inequalities and discrimination in
education and career opportunities that still pertain today and are
discussed in the DfES's* Aiming High *of 2003. The Eggleston report
was significant for its uncompromising presentation of evidence*

and for its far-reaching recommendations summarised here, along with excerpts from the introduction.

Equally uncompromising was the ethnographic study by a young black PhD student, Cecile Wright – now a Professor herself. In her important chapter she revealed disturbing evidence of racial prejudice and discrimination in schools along two specific lines. She showed how in one school students were adopting resistance strategies to what they freely told her was constant racism from teachers and white peers, such as speaking Patois and 'moving around the school together'. Her study of the examination banding at another school showed clearly that the colour of a student's skin was a more dominant factor in teachers' selection for exam bands than were the marks the students had attained.

Introduction

The Department of Education and Science funded a three and a half year research project at the University of Keele. It was directed by Professor S.J. Eggleston; the researchers were Madhu Anjali., David Dunn and Terry Leander. Beginning 1 April 1981 it consisted of a study of students at 23 schools in six local education authorities in the North, the Midlands and Greater London. The students comprised a 'quasi-random' sample taken from mixed-ability tutor groups in each school. They were first approached two terms before they reached the statutory school-leaving age in 1982, and again one year later. Other research activities included approaches to careers officers, teachers, parents, Manpower Service Commission officers and employers. Analyses of school records, examination results and other relevant data were undertaken.

The aims of the research were expressed in the project proposal as follows:

> It is envisaged that the project would be able to present information of very considerable value to those concerned with the development of education in the multicultural society of the 1980s. There would be enhancement of our knowledge of the link between educational provision and ethnic group membership, aspirations, achievement, and employment. A new and clearer map of the distribution of opportunity for and between young people of the various ethnic groups would become available that could facilitate the development of provision for

both minority and majority groups. Areas of special opportunity and disadvantage and the ways in which these are related to distinctive occupational and social characteristics would be illuminated. Areas where educational provision had been particularly successful would be identified and these could be juxtaposed against other areas where problems were in evidence. In particular it is likely that the study will be able to identify previously covert areas of opportunity which, when more fully known, may become more widely available. Most funda-mentally it is to be hoped that the project would illuminate the major unevennesses between supply and demand of labour and educational opportunity which so disadvantage many minority groups and provide information that could allow the development of policies leading to a more effective matching between opportunity and need than at present exists.

... Between October 1979 and October 1982, when our students might have been able to look for work, unemployment for under-18 year old school leavers more than doubled. Increases in unemploy-ment always has disproportionately severe effects on black people in Britain. Furthermore, young black people face severe difficulties in obtaining work in all circumstances: At every stage, and by virtually every test which is applied, black and Asian racial disadvantage is in evidence: in the search for work; in the kinds of jobs found; in the gaps between job aspirations and job attainments; in representation among the ranks of the unemployed. The additive effects of labour market forces and racial discrimination in employment provide an inescapable background for this study, affecting both its data and the conclusions to which they lead.

NOTE: The term 'racism' is widely used in current literature in this field and in the comments of our respondents. Throughout the report we use the term to describe attitudes more fundamental, more con-sistent and often more widespread than those usually labelled as racial prejudice. These are seen to lead to a range of practices, con-scious and well as unconscious, in the life of schools that act to the detriment of ethnic minority pupils. We do not use the term to indicate a conscious or articulated ideology.

Conclusions and Recommendations
Introduction

If there is a single theme that runs through this report, it is the determination of very large numbers of young people from ethnic
minority groups to persevere with their education in the hope of
obtaining their desired occupations. This persistence is evident in
many ways: in homework and extra school work, investing time in
school sixth-forms, colleges of further education and part-time
courses and the keen desire to enter higher education.

This determination is frequently associated with occupational ambitions that are no higher than those of white pupils in the same
schools and colleges. And even where these ambitions are higher,
they are almost always appropriately linked to the qualifications being realistically pursued by the young people. It is this theme of
persistence and willingness to invest both time and money for self
improvement which is so pervasively evident throughout.

There are social processes in schools and in society at large that work
to counteract the efforts of these young people. In schools, both at
and below sixth form level, ethnic minority pupils may be placed on
courses and entered for examinations at levels below those appropriate for their abilities and ambitions. Teachers may be unwilling to
accept the existence of these processes, or even to redress them where
they are aware of them. And when schools fail, young black people
can find it difficult to enter colleges of further education.

In society at large, the effects of racial discrimination upon employment prospects appear to be severe. Even when young black people
do attain appropriate qualifications, they do not obtain jobs in equal
proportion to whites either before or after participating in schemes.
We cannot report extensively on the experiences of young people in
this situation: only small numbers in our cohort had left education.
We have however, using both local and national data, outlined the
incidence of unemployment amongst young black people.

The research cohort

The project's conclusions on the experiences of young people in
their fifth year at school are in the main derived from a cohort of 593
young people. Approximately half these respondents were white.

The group included 157 pupils of South Asian and 110 of Afro-Caribbean ethnic origins. They attended 23 comprehensive secondary schools in six LEAs in Bedford, Birmingham, Bradford and London. Most respondents, black and white, were born in Britain: almost all the others had lived here for more than five years.

Aspirations

In their fifth year at school, more black than white young people were expecting to undertake a one year sixth form course, usually to enhance O level or CSE stocks, and a greater proportion of Afro-Caribbean pupils wanted to go to colleges of further education. More respondents of both white and South Asian backgrounds were expecting to take GCE A levels, and the latter group were more likely to be envisaging spending three further years doing so. A high proportion of all groups expected to resit their fifth year public examinations in the following year in school or college. It is probable that some of the enthusiasm to continue full-time education sprang from a lack of confidence about employment and a desire not to face negative experiences.

Very few fifth year pupils reported having had work experience at school, and only half the black respondents had worked part-time or assisted a family business, compared to three-quarters of the whites. Afro-Caribbean pupils unable to obtain part-time work were significantly more likely to have wanted to do so.

Examinations

In public examinations at sixteen-plus, there were few differences in the results achieved by pupils of white and South Asian ethnic origin, though white girls and Asian boys gained, overall, slightly higher grades. Afro-Caribbean girls achieved grades similar to white boys, but Afro-Caribbean boys got the lowest grades in the cohort though they were only half as likely as other groups to be entered for any GCE O level.

These differences in examination performance do not necessarily reflect the abilities of the young people. And, as levels of attainment differed between and within local authorities, the order of attainment between groups did not remain constant. Most Afro-Caribbean pupils in the cohort were attending a small number of schools in only two of the six LEAs. Furthermore, the ethnographic study conducted in the two additional schools in a separate LEA suggested that special factors might operate in some schools to the disadvantage of Afro-Caribbean pupils. If teachers hold views antagonistic to particular racial groups and if in any resulting conflict these teachers are supported by the authority structure of their schools, this is likely to be detrimental to the attainments of most if not all pupils of that group. *Where racial prejudice operates among teachers, low examination achievements could be an even less adequate than usual indication of a young person's occupational capacity.*

Finding work

White young people in our cohort were more likely than ethnic minority pupils to leave school at sixteen. Of our respondents who had left school, whites were more likely to be employed: indeed none of our black male respondents held a full-time job. White respondents also spent less time before getting their first job, and had held more jobs overall – even when we exclude the number of those who had never been employed. Although white young people had made more applications for jobs, the differences were not statistically significant, and disappeared when we removed from consideration girls who had not applied for any jobs at all. The unemployed black respondents were more likely than the white to be registered as unemployed. Given their employment predicaments, it is not surprising that black respondents were much more likely than whites to wish they had stayed at school or gone to college.

Continuing Education

Black respondents in continuing education were also willing to invest a great deal of persistence in the pursuit of qualifications. Half the black young people leaving school after a one year sixth-form course were intending to go to college afterwards, compared with less than one fifth of whites. About a third of respondents of South Asian origin and Afro-Caribbean girls were envisaging spending at least three years before taking A level examinations, and a greater proportion were hoping to get A levels.

Black students were on similar levels of course in both schools and colleges – with about one third taking vocational examinations in schools and taking or aiming to take A levels in colleges. White students were distributed differently. Few were taking vocational course in schools or A levels in colleges of further education.

Our analysis of students in further education cannot be conclusive because of the low numbers of respondents. There is certainly a suggestion that Afro-Caribbean young people had found it difficult to get into college, while those who had actually succeeded had done so after more applications and more rejections. We found no evidence of any specially devised 'access' routes and noted that black young people tended to obtain details of college opportunities by informal and incomplete methods.

A greater proportion of black students hoped to enter higher education. Nearly two thirds of Asian respondents in continuing education had this in mind. Again we found no awareness of special 'access' programmes. Both the students aiming for higher education and those intending to look for work seemed to have considerable faith in the ability of education to get them a better job.

It is the distress associated with unemployment and the insecurity of low status jobs that many young black people are seeking to avoid in struggling for qualifications and skilled or non-manual occupations.

Our report was addressed to the Department of Education and Science, so detailed recommendations to alleviate racial discrimination in employment would not be appropriate. But continuing education alone can by no means remove racial – or other – forms of discrimination from the labour market. It is a far wider social problem, one of great urgency – as indicated by Lord Scarman.

Recommendations
(Original emphasis throughout)

Schools
1. Black pupils give the schools a major vote of confidence by staying on in very large numbers. They do so for reasons arising from keen occupational aspirations which are seldom un-realistic, mixed possibly with fundamental doubts about their

own capabilities and a desire not to expose themselves to failure in the labour market. We recommend that all schools take more active steps to *justify and reward* this high rate of staying on. In particular we recommend very careful *planning of the curriculum* and organisation for the 16 + that takes full account of their ambitions, motivations and their uncertainties. The opportunities are great; students are present by choice rather than obligation and, in most cases there are smaller class sizes allowing more individual teaching. Yet schools sometimes offer little more than a repeat performance of the situations in which many of these pupils have already failed or achieved minimally. They require something more imaginative than a programme of CSE/O level resits not impossible in most schools. A programme of pre-A level courses, vocationally oriented) level courses and some components of the new spectrum of technical and vocational school leaving examinations being developed within the context of TVEI may offer pupils more attractive options. In addition to the examination work, a programme of non-examination activities that explore vocational, community and recreational opportunities could be devised, in consultation with the students, to help them to maximise their own resources and those of the neighbourhood.

2. We recommend that schools pay particular attention to their *procedures of allocation to sets, streams, bands* and other work and ability groups so that they fully recognise not only the existing achievement but also the potential of their students. There is evidence in our report to indicate that this is by no means always done. Although labelling theory is fallible it still offers a valuable explanation of much of the profile of expectations that surround children and teachers. Faulty allocation can lead to faulty achievement and it seems to be Afro-Caribbean children who suffer most severely in this process.

3. We recommend that schools carefully examine their *procedures for examination entries and allocation to examination groups* to ensure fair treatment of all ethnic groups and also to ensure that individual pupils are given the fullest opportunity to attain the highest level qualification of which they are capable. Chapter 10

shows the differentially low entry rates of black young people but indicates that factors suggesting that academic potential is not fully recognised due to overt and covert expectations, traditions and 'ethos'. The evidence of higher proportional exam success rate of black young people in further education as opposed to schools reinforces this view and our recommendation.

4. Chapter 12 and previous chapters give evidence than unemployed young blacks were disadvantaged by lack of confidence despite high occupational motivation and enthusiasm for educational qualifications. We recommend that schools make a particular effort in their curriculum arrangements to ensure that they are offering all children the best chance to identify and develop the most marketable skills appropriate to their chances in the labour market. We recommend that schools seek to *identify and help to develop the capacities of their minority group pupils*. More schools might allow their pupils to return after an unsatisfactory trial of the labour market. We recognise in making this recommendation that there is a thin dividing line between emphasising strengths and building upon them and identifying differences and stereotyping them. With equal conviction *we recommend schools not to 'ghettoise' their ethnic minority pupils by providing them with a 'soft option' curriculum* in which they can succeed. This can do no more than substitute low attainment in mainstream marketable skills for high attainment in non-marketable skills. We recommend schools to *deliver a curriculum relevant to the potentials of black and white children* and which recognises their full range of capabilities.

5. We recommend schools to pay careful attention to the *quality control of the experience of their black students*. On some occasions we found it difficult to obtain a clear picture of the participation in the curriculum, of the results of tests and written assignments. We are convinced that the best interests of all children are served by careful recording of achievement which can be used for enhanced diagnosis and guidance and the identification of potential.

6. We were sometimes told of instances of 'bad behaviour' by black students. But we were also reminded that bad behaviour can be a

means of communication by children especially when they are frustrated by low achievement and low status. But whatever the cause when black children behave badly, formal punishment can often reinforce negative racial stereotypes and hence lower the expectations of black pupils achieving well. This is particularly so if they are seen as receiving unequal treatment. We recommend schools to take particular care in their *strategies of punishing black pupils*. This applies not only to 'in school' punishments such as withdrawal of status but also to exclusion and withdrawal of support for employment or continuing education.

7. Despite much advocacy some schools and colleges seemed to have made relatively little progress in involving black parents particularly in decisions about careers. Yet the potential for a full and effective parental involvement is to be seen in our study where we report on the commitment of some groups of black parents both to the school and their influence on the education and future of their children. We recommend all schools to reinforce their efforts to *inform and involve all parents*.

8. In some schools the *use of English language is seen to have an effect on placement*. Unless and until children are able to utilise standard varieties of English usage they may be held back from a number of the more demanding and rewarding courses. This is understandable but it contrasts strikingly with most British universities and polytechnics where overseas students with modest command of English regularly obtain Masters and PhD degrees. Such students with only a relatively modest initial command of English find that their fluency increases most effectively as they work in their chosen subject. We recommend schools to consider similar approaches with ethnic minority children.

9. The TVEI in schools had not begun during our study period so we had no opportunity to assess its efficacy. However study of the scheme and its subsequent operation leads us to believe that many aspects of the scheme may be specially relevant to the needs of some black children. This is likely to be particularly the case in the 16 + years of the scheme (yet to be reached in any school). *We recommend that all schools developing the TVEI*

should pay particular attention to the ways in which black children may benefit. It could well be that these could provide more marketable attainments than the CSE or CEE courses undertaken by some sixth form and college pupils.

10. A number of the schools we studied offered work experience programmes for children. These schemes involved a variety of factory visits, simulation, work study and other approaches. We recommend that schools using such approaches pay particular attention to *familiarising employers and potential employers with the full potential and capabilities of black children* and that all other contacts of the school be also used for this purpose.

11. Anti-racist guidelines are now being issued by some local educational authorities. Although our evidence is spasmodic, it suggests that such guidelines can point the way to understanding the needs and sensitivities of the ethnic minority groups more fully and we recommend schools to take anti-racist guidelines seriously. In some schools there may still be genuinely racist teachers. *We recommend that racist teachers be given a clear opportunity to consider whether or not they are still suitable to be members of the profession.*

All this is not to say that the schools must become obsessionally sensitive. If teachers and – pupils are – aware of the issues, they will be able to handle the prejudice that frequently occurs in the playground, the community and the workplace in a way that helps both black and white children to be unharmed by it and ultimately to diminish it.

12. *We recommend that all teachers recognise that there are many ways in which their responsibility for guidance and encouragement and support may be shown.* Our evidence suggests that many young black children, though having a realistic appraisal of their prospects, lack confidence in their own judgement and fail to get the reassurances that are apparently experienced by white children. This lack of encouragement may occur not through overt action by teachers but through the 'hidden curriculum' that regulates behaviour both in and out of school. Some black young people may need explicit assistance in coming to terms with aspects that other children have learnt implicitly.

Furthermore, the way in which *'diagnostic' guidance is offered needs to be especially sensitive* so that correct guidance may not be ignored for incorrect reasons.

13. To conclude this section of recommendations to schools and teachers we would urge the fundamental truth that schools and their teachers must start with the child where he is. To paraphrase the precept of Bernstein, 'if the consciousness of the teacher is to be in the mind of the child then first of all the consciousness of the child must be in the mind of the teacher'.

Further Education

As with schools, the experience of further education is a crucial aspect of the educational and pre-vocational experience of many black young people. In our sample we found black young people were twice as likely to go to college as whites – this was even more true of Asian boys and Afro-Caribbean girls. Yet there was much evidence of ignorance and uncertainty about the opportunities provided by further education.

1. We recommend that *further education establishments present the opportunities they offer more clearly and directly to black and white young people.* Many seemed to rely on informal and incomplete information about further education – a mixture of street and conventional wisdom. There are many ways in which this presentation may be enhanced through link courses, open days, better promotional material. The specific solutions will vary in accordance with the resources and capabilities of the institution and the needs of its potential clients. This recommendation is applicable not only to full-time courses but also to the part-time courses favoured by many black young people both working and unemployed. The modest programme of access courses developed by Millins as part of a DES project based at Ealing College of Higher Education demonstrated how careful bridging could provide a path between low formal attainment and university and polytechnic education. There seems a similar need for access provision to bridge the much smaller gap between low or non-existent school attainment and further education. At the moment this gap tends to be bridged by a further year of resits in the schools. We recommend that *further*

education establishments take the initiative to develop appropriate access courses in liaison with the schools.

2. We recommend that *further education institutions should emphasise that they are first chance institutions for those for whom school may have been irrelevant or an experience of failure* and not merely second-chance institutions where an alternative venue is offered to take O and A levels, and similar 'in school' qualifications.

    Chapter 11 showed that many young blacks tend to use further education for academic and vocational purposes, in contrast to whites who use it for predominantly vocational purposes. Yet some black youths receive a more vocationally-linked further education than received by whites. If further education institutions can be more alert to these issues and solve the problems of presentation, access and content, then they will be able to offer young people a far fuller choice at 16 +.

3. Closely associated with all this is the need for further education establishments themselves to reappraise their views about the potential achievement of young black students. In the recommendations to schools we have drawn attention to the distance between the low expectations of black students by some teachers and the high expectations which surround black students from overseas who come to establishments of higher education and successfully obtain higher degrees. It has been put to us that some young blacks have only one fundamental disadvantage in reaching advanced qualifications; they have lived in Britain instead of overseas. We recommend *colleges of further education to be alert to the full potential of their black students*. The suggestion of higher thresholds of admission for young black students in some colleges of further education (Chapter 11) adds urgency to this recommendation.

Careers Service

The Careers Service is a major influence on the educational and vocational experience of young people of ethnic minority groups but there was much evidence of the inconsistent delivery of the Service to a number of black young people. Our general recommendations follow. A number of detailed recommendations are also included in the statements from ethnic minority specialist careers officers in the Appendix.

1. ... We recommend that all *Careers Services be required to adopt clear and uniform statistical procedures* to ensure a true local and national data base.

2. ... We recommend that the *Careers Service persevere in its attempts to ensure complete coverage* in the interests of the young and of society at large. Our other recommendations depend upon and reinforce this central need.

3. We recommend that the *Careers Service give considerably more attention to the ways in which young people are prepared for interviews*, perhaps by finding ways in which young people can learn about the world of work before their interview. ...

4. Yet another feature of the situation is that *some black young people may need a longer time scale to identify their opportunities*. In part this may arise from cultural isolation, particularly from the 'job network'. (Most black children still obtain most job information from informal contacts). It may also arise from the lack in confidence in their capabilities, particularly faced with white successes. ...

5. We encountered suggestions that not all Careers Officers fully recognise the extent of racial discrimination in the labour market and that some held stereotyped or preconceived views about the roles and capabilities of black young people. We recommend that the *Careers Service refines its procedures for not only recognising but also acting upon evidence of discrimination*. We also recommend that the *Service institutes more effective procedures for monitoring referrals to training schemes and employment interviews*, to assist young black people to receive equal opportunities to acquire both marketable skills and paid employment.

6. Associated with this we recommend a considerable extension in the arrangements for *in-service training within the Careers Service* in which appropriate aspects of race awareness training play a proper part.

7. We recommend that the *Careers Service literature* made available by the Careers Service is not only comprehensive and readily available to all young people but also that it is *carefully scrutinised* to avoid presenting stereotypes of racial differentiation in employment. ...

Local Education Authorities

The Local Education Authorities, through their provision of schools, further educational establishments and Careers Services and advisory services and welfare provision, play a crucial part in the experiences and achievements of minority group adolescents. Our main recommendation to them is that they seek to implement the recommendations we made to their schools and colleges. In addition, we offer the following:

1. We recommend that *all authorities develop guidelines for their institutions and staffs to help eliminate discriminatory, prejudicial and racist behaviour.* Our evidence suggests that some teachers need to be reminded of the implications and consequences of their behaviour in their work with children from a range of ethnic groups. Such guidelines also perform a further service for the Local Education Authorities; they provide a standard against which discriminatory behaviour can be judged.

    We recommend that all Local Education Authorities develop strategies to *identify materials in the schools which convey discriminatory messages* and, in particular that literature which indicates differentiated occupation roles between black and white people should not be available to influence the occupational decisions of black or white young people.

3. We recommend that Local Education Authorities recognise the *gulf that exists between many low achieving young people in the schools and their aspirations for entry to further education.* This gulf is not always unbridgable and we recommend that all Local Authorities seek to develop a range of access routes for entry to their further education establishments.

4. Such developments as we have recommended for the schools cannot take place without the support of a committed local Inspectorial or Advisory service and we recommend that *all*

Local Authorities take steps to ensure that their whole advisory service (and not just those members specifically concerned with multi-ethnic education) are fully aware of what is needed and seek to implement changes. This could include the development of relevant in-service courses, guidance and counselling to individual teachers and to school staffs as a whole and an alert presence in the school.

5. We recommend that all *Local Authorities take urgent steps to explore the workings of local Careers Services,* to ensure an effective delivery to all young people.

Department of Education and Science

Although our study did not directly explore the actions of central government we feel it appropriate to address a number of our recommendations directly to the Department of Education and Science. They are:

1. Existing methods of assessment are not always appropriate to record the achievement of minority ethnic groups and to diagnose their potential. We recommend the Department to urge the *School Examination Council to bear in mind the position of candidates from ethnic minorities in renewing criteria for examinations at 16+.*

2. Not all schools provide a curriculum for all their pupils that is effectively directed to identifying and developing their marketable skills. We recommend that new *School Curriculum Development Committee be urged to pay particular attention to this aspect of curriculum.*

3. *There is an urgent need for fuller information on the activities of the 18-19 year old population.* For the most part these young people have completed schooling, further education or participation in MSC schemes. Remarkably little is known about this age group of young people and we recommend that the Department, in liaison with other relevant Ministries, seeks ways of rectifying this information gap. This could provide a more useful guide than we have presently to the consequences of various kinds of educational experience.

4. There is a need for a *concerted programme of in-service training for teachers and careers officers* concerned with the placement and guidance of young people from the ethnic minority groups. Wherever possible it is desirable that employers participate in such training. It is recommended that the prevocational programmes initiated in Circular 3/83 and Circular 4/84 courses be augmented to pay particular attention to this need.

5. Not all schools have considered sufficiently the opportunities presented to them by the young black students who present themselves for continuing education in the schools after the minimum leaving age. We recommend that the *DES and HMI give urgent attention to ways in which schools may be helped to develop appropriate provision.*

6. We recommend that *continuing pressure be placed on teacher training establishments to ensure that all students develop an appropriate sensitivity and perceptiveness for working with minority group adolescents.* This could include experience of good practice in schools and colleges and HMI guidance may be useful in identifying such placements in some areas.

7. More generally we recommend that all *published reports by DES and HMI* ranging from those on individual schools through to major reports on curriculum and organisation *should be written with an awareness of the special needs to which we have drawn attention* and that where appropriate, specific mention of alleviatory strategies should be offered.

[Recommendations were also made to the Manpower Services Commission]

In this lengthy series of recommendations we have drawn attention to many ways in which the quality of educational experience offered to young members of ethnic minority groups may be enhanced and in so doing, enhance their educational and vocational experience. Inevitably such recommendations emphasise the changes needed. All are based upon shortcomings that became evident as we worked with young people, teachers, careers advisers, Manpower Services Commission officers, employers and many other participants in the education service. But we make the recommendations with confidence because we also have evidence, clear in our report, that there are many examples of good practice in which the experience of young people, both black and white, is successful, fulfilling and rewarding. We believe that our recommendations, if adopted, could make this satisfactory state of affairs far more widely available.

Some of the changes we suggest require additional costs and resources. We hope that they are recognised as of sufficient importance to merit funds even in present economic conditions. But most changes needed are in the perception and attitude on the part of individuals and require no new money. Moreover, such changes, by enhancing human capability and diminishing the waste of human resources, may result in substantial economic gain.

It has been said that schools and colleges cannot fundamentally change the labour market; they cannot eradicate structural unemployment. But there is some limited evidence, confirmed in our report, that schools can enhance the employability of their young people and that this may have a small but beneficial effect on the labour market. Some schools might even develop entrepreneurial characteristics in their young people so leading them to create their own employment opportunities. But of even greater importance is that achievement of a number of schools in helping to create a more just and equitable distribution of opportunities in our society. We believe that our recommendations can facilitate this process. Achieving greater justice between the races in these ways may well be the way in which the education service can best contribute to the diminution of racial tension and bitterness.

References

Brah, A. K. and Golding, P. (1983) *The Transition from School to Work among Young Asians in Leicester* Centre for Mass Communications Research University of Leicester, Leicester 5. 1.

The Brixton Disorders, 10-12 April 1981: Report of an Inquiry by the Rt Hon The Lord Scarman OBE (1981) HMSO London.

9

Can Anti-racist Education survive the 1988 Act?

The 1988 Education Act extended and embedded the divisive and exclusionary drive of the 1986 Act. In MCT Multicultural Teaching *8.3, John Eggleston looked back at the initial impact of the two Acts and asked:*

Can anti-racist education survive the 1988 Education Act?

My position is simple, familiar and positive. Good anti-racist teaching is the key to good education. Every report confirms this. The Smith and Tomlinson report for the Policy Studies Institute (1989), the ILEA report on Black Achievement, (published just before the end of ILEA 1990), the work that Barry Troyna and Richard Hatcher are currently undertaking all demonstrate that good anti-racist teaching with a real belief in its efficacy, can ensure that so – called underachieving groups can achieve. Their work shows that there is no necessary correlation between race and achievement. Individual achievement varies, of course, but these variations are not imposed by race any more than they are by gender or class. If I had the slightest doubt it would have been erased by the evidence we have assembled at Warwick University for the Further Education Unit on the Education of Unemployed Black Adults. In a range of self-help black-led groups that we worked with, hundreds of black young people who had failed at school were achieving highly in professional and vocational qualifications, employment, degree and diploma programmes. We hope to be able to publish this report very shortly, following final approval from the Further Education Unit.

All the progress that is being made is likely to be impeded, if not arrested, by the implementation of the Education Reform Act. NAME (National Association for Multicultural Education) has been saying this for years now, as has almost every other body with a real concern for the education of young people black and white. Miraculously, even Mrs Thatcher now seems to have realised it, albeit incompletely, in her *Sunday Telegraph* interview on 15 March 1990 – at a stroke, she has abolished testing at 7 and 11 in all seven of the non-core foundation subjects of the National Curriculum, having recognised the difficulty and potential injustice that was likely. The National Union of Teachers has come out clearly about the near impossibility of implementing the testing arrangements made law by the Act, and Education Officers up and down the country are demonstrating that it is virtually impossible to make Local Management of Schools work effectively and yet still retain the crucial services provided centrally by the local authorities. In Avon, even the school secretaries are up in arms about the impossibility of implementing the Education Reform Act effectively within their schools.

Let me mention a few of the major areas of difficulty. Not surprisingly, I'll start with Local Management of Schools. The sharp reduction in funding that this is bringing about in virtually all schools regardless of the communities they serve is public knowledge. The problem is, of course, particularly acute in schools with substantial ethnic minority populations; the classic case of Cabot School in Bristol is but one of the many examples where a school previously supported by substantial LEA enhancement is facing draconian cuts in its budget. Added to the erosion in Section XI funding, the effects are dramatic. But why don't schools wishing to provide generously for the needs of black children use their new freedom to make appropriate provision? Alas, it is not that simple. Not only are those funds reduced but the pressure on all schools to ensure high recruitment and retention of pupils is likely to push them in a different direction. Every school, if it is to ensure that it is able to obtain even a reasonable funding basis, has to fight to keep its numbers at a high level.

The sovereign parents will now control the numbers of pupils who walk through the school gates each morning and thereby determine the size of the school budget.

The way to win these parents' minds is, increasingly, to show not only high levels of achievement, (as measured by the results of the Standardised Attainment Tasks) but also to provide the goodies that are now seen to be the hallmark of affluent schools – computers, and other electronic hardware and software, resources and facilities of all kinds. It is on such items that schools will have to spend as much of their funding if they are to stay viable. Our research in the West Midlands has shown very clearly that black parents, understandably, will favour the schools that the white parents favour and many have sound evidence to justify their preferences (Eggleston and Sadler, 1988, Eggleston and Lashley 1989). So it is unlikely that schools will be able to invest heavily in the kind of support systems that have previously been so beneficial for their Black pupils. The remnants of Local Education Authority support for anti-racist education are likely to be further eroded by the current Government-led encouragement to schools to press for even higher proportions of the education rather than the Local Education Authority's budget to be made available to them. Indeed it would not be too great an extrapolation of the Education Secretary's recent pronouncements to predict an end to Local Education Authorities as we now know them within the next 4-5 years. It requires little further predictive capability to recognise that the LEA anti-racist and multicultural support teams would be some of the earliest casualties in the process.

Closely associated with Local Management of Schools is the parents' new 'freedom of choice'. There has always been the possibility that parental choice would covertly create an apartheid situation in schools, with many white parents electing to send their pupils to the 'all white' schools. What has not been realised until now has been that the preference based on this kind of ethnic apartheid would not only be visible but also overt. The case whereby Cleveland Education Authority has allowed a parent to exercise choice explicitly for these reasons, a choice that has now been endorsed by the Department of Education and Science, raises a wholly new dimension which adds dramatically to the racist implications of the 1988 Act.

The National Curriculum itself is, as we already know, fraught with problems. There is some hope for a genuinely multi-ethnic perspective in the reports of the Working Groups on Mathematics, Science, English and Technology. Perhaps the most encouraging feature is the emphasis on non-standard English in the English document. But overall these concessions to a multi-ethnic dimension are small, and in the context of the whole reports marginal. Moreover, it is difficult to see those elements in the trial materials currently being produced in some of the curriculum areas. Even schools with the best intentions may find it hard to devote any significant attention to the multi-ethnic dimension in their curriculum and in this way much of what has been achieved in recent years is likely to be lost. In time, there will be cross-curricular themes and one of them will be multi-cultural, but these are yet to be glimpsed and their implementation may be a long time ahead – if ever.

The Standardised Attainment Tasks are perhaps one of the major areas of concern. Research after research has demonstrated that children from ethnic minorities, particularly those who do not have the majority language as their mother tongue, are likely to do less well than mainstream speakers of standard English. There is here, however, a ray of hope: the tests could effectively demonstrate the true capability, of black as well as white children. There is much evidence showing that teachers, even if 'well intentioned' often fail to recognise the true ability of black children and regularly place them in lower attaining streams and examination courses than they have the capability to occupy. If black children and their parents, as a result of Standardised Attainment Tasks have convincing, negotiable evidence of their capability then this discrimination should be less likely to occur. However, the recent statement by Mrs Thatcher, focusing the testing on English, Maths and Science only at 7 and 11 may turn out to be disadvantageous because it is precisely in these areas, often wedded to traditional teaching and assessment, that black children may do less well, whereas in some of the other foundation areas they might have had a more open chance to demonstrate high achievement and potential. And, perhaps most fundamentally, the emphasis on Standardised Attainment Tasks particularly in the basic subjects is likely to minimise the impressive non-assessible achievements in anti-racist education that many teachers have devoted their efforts to in recent years. Schools as well as children are likely to be increasingly assessed and valued on a narrow, even blinkered, curriculum.

Underlining all this is the question of ideology. The Ministerial position is consistent – all that is needed is good teaching of black and white young people and obsession with anti-racism, with its 'loony left' connotations, is simply a distraction. Their concern with good teaching sounds disconcertingly like my own concern. But there is a fundamental difference: for me good teaching cannot exist without a sound, coherent anti-racist perspective. The Ministerial team had a field day over the publication of the Smith and Tomlinson Report (1989) by the Policy Studies Institute. This report was seen to indicate that their thesis was sound and much play was made on the fact that achievement was low in a number of schools with strong anti-racist commitment. The reason for their low achievement was, of course, seen to be their preoccupation with this time-consuming ideological distraction. The exultant commentary ignored two basic features which were clearly to be seen in the report. The first was that a number of the high achieving schools also had anti-racist policies and that a number of the low achieving schools did not, and, secondly, that in many inner city schools black children could and should do better than the norm for the often low-aspiring white children who shared their schools. To suggest that the highest level of white attainment in any school must also mark the upper level of achievement for black children is perhaps one of the most oppressive forms of racism and racist comment but seems to have passed un-challenged.

To ensure real achievement, it is imperative to develop an anti-racist National Curriculum to match our enthusiasm for anti-racist teaching. There are a number of pressure groups that are working to achieve this – NAME itself, the Greystoke Group in Manchester, ARTEN, CARE, all recognise that the key to achievement is empowerment. But this is not empowerment of some at the expense of others. If teacher expectations are not to be discriminatory, empowering some and disempowering others, then we must recognise the fundamental truth that power is not a scarce commodity but one that it can be enjoyed and shared. Power is only in short supply if we care to make it so and create artificial shortages. Until we recognise this and erase the expectations of, or even the fear of, wide distribution of power within society, achievement itself will be in short supply.

The path we have to tread within the Educational Reform Act is hard but we can still win. We must make the Act work for anti-racist education and achievement for all and use every means to adapt it, modify it, exploit it, and to make it happen. We must not wait for a new Education Act, however attractive this may be. If we do, then tens of thousands of children will have missed their chance while we are negotiating and acting politically. There is a short-term goal as well as a medium term one. We must work towards both if we are to do justice to the children, black and white, currently in our schools.

References

Eggleston, J and Sadler, E. (1988) *The Participation of Ethnic Minority pupils in TVEI* London, The Training Agency

Eggleston, J. and Lashley, H. (1989) *An Examination of the Educational and Vocational Experience of Young People from Ethnic Minorities in Warwickshire*, Warwickshire County Council.

Smith, D. and Tomlinson. S. (1989) *The School Effect*, London, Policy Studies Institute.

10

The Challenge for Teachers

John Eggleston believed that The Challenge for Teachers *(1992) was his most underrated book – and one of his best. Part of a series for students,* Introduction to Education, *it was commissioned by the overall editor, Jonathan Solity, a colleague at University of Warwick who drew on the expertise in John's Department of Education for several volumes in the series.*

We believe that if every student leaning to teach, then and through to today, understood and abided by the principles and precepts of this wise book which overarched the series, the lot of many children in education in the UK would have been significantly enhanced, along with their achievement.

After a brief introductory chapter, John moves promptly to key issues.

Issues of social class, gender and race
This chapter reviews the ways in which differences in social class, gender and race can influence children's achievement. It reviews key concepts of socialisation, inner- and other-directedness, restricted and elaborated language codes and social and cultural reproduction. In particular it outlines how positive rather than passive teacher roles may be achieved.

Key teacher tasks
*   Trying to ensure that one discovers the capabilities of all children.

119

- Taking care that one's judgements are not influenced by negative expectations about social class, gender or race.

- Building upon what capabilities the children already have, never suggesting that what they bring (especially in the way of language) is valueless.

- Remembering that differences established or reinforced in school may determine almost all aspects of a child's future and, collectively, play a large part in determining future social structure.

Children come to school with different physical, mental and emotional capabilities. They also come with a bewildering variety of expectations and attitudes that may enhance or diminish the full realisation of their capability. These expectations and attitudes are largely a product of their social background and spring from the value systems of their parents, their extended families and the adults and other children in their communities. They are important not only because they have a formative effect on the children but also because they interact with the expectations and attitudes of teachers. Often teachers, despite much effort to the contrary, end up by reinforcing the differentiating consequences of these underlying values, not infrequently to the disadvantage of children.

There are three main categories into which these underlying value systems, with their representative attitudes and expectations, may be placed: social class, gender, and race. Each of these areas is considered in detail in other volumes in this series. Here their effect on work in the classroom and hence their crucial importance in the work of the teacher is examined.

Social Class

A clear example is provided at the outset of schooling. Let us imagine two children entering school from different ends of the social class structure. They are coming into the reception class of a first school serving a catchment area that spans the social spectrum.

On the first morning Kate, from an affluent suburban home, arrives with Kylie, from a much less affluent inner-city family. They enter a well-equipped modern classroom supervised by a teacher who is enthusiastic to help all the children in her class to maximise their capability. Yet Kate will start with many advantages. She will be familiar with the equipment, having almost certainly met it in her home and pre-school playgroup. She will be relaxed with teachers, as she and her parents are likely to know teachers socially and to 'speak the same language'. So she is likely to use her new environment effectively and immediately and to be posting the bricks in the correct slots in the postbox without waiting to be asked. Meanwhile, Kylie has probably been sent to school with the injunction 'Make sure you do what the teacher tells you', and is waiting patiently for the teacher to tell her when to use the unfamiliar equipment for the first time. It is very difficult for the teacher, armed with her developmental checklist, to resist evaluating Kate as 'bright and quick' and Kylie as 'dull and slow' in the first few hours, when the crucial early (and often persistent) diagnoses are made. The diagnosis is very likely to be reinforced by Kate's greater familiarity with books in the home and the strong probability that her parents have already taught her to read.

Gender

Similar pre-judgements are all too easy to make on gender issues. Boys, encouraged in home and community to be more dominant, assertive and adventurous and to enjoy approval for such behaviour, will behave differently in the classroom from girls, who have often received a very different early encouragement. In particular, as most teachers acknowledge, boys tend to be much more effective in claiming teachers' attention, with predictable consequences for teachers' evaluation.

Race

Much the same can happen when children from different ethnic backgrounds enter the classroom: their different languages and cultural backgrounds may make it less easy for them to relate to the 'mainstream' knowledge and understanding they are offered. In consequence their achievement may be seen to be lower and their capabilities in their own home language and culture may go unrecognised. The point is well made by Francis O'Reilly, writing in *The Independent* on 13 September 1990:

The Maths teacher introduces the student teacher to the class and briefs her. Before leaving, she points out a girl sitting on the back row and says, 'Oh, by the way, Jhamari won't understand anything. Give her some additions to do.'

In French, where they have to label parts of the body, Jhamari steals a glance at her neighbour's book and earns the snarling response, 'Buzz off, stop copying!' In Humanities they are discussing the Reformation and Jhamari is asked to draw a picture of Henry VIII. In science 'sir' need not keep a wary eye on her as she sits, mute, devoid of mischief and curiosity. She goes from class to class in a dream – eyes not fearful or expectant, but dead.

Jhamari is not handicapped or mentally disturbed. She is simply Bengali. She and many like her go through the school day and the school year as through a great sterile desert, uncomprehending, shut off, neither gaining nor giving. What potential they have is never realised, because it goes unrecognised ...

The presence of silent passengers in the classroom means a failure of education, wasted childhoods and demoralised or desensitised teachers. It should at very least become an immediate focus of research, debate and policy.

The crucial point in these three simplified examples of class, gender and race is that whilst the capability and potential of the children may be similar, the teacher's evaluation is likely to be different and to have crucial consequences in subsequent actual achievement. This is because of the formative nature both of children's self-image and of teachers' expectations. In addition, other children in the class-room are quick to reinforce the teacher's expectations. These self-fulfilling prophecies form a central theme of subsequent chapters.

We must emphasise very strongly, however, that this is not an argu-ment for 'putting down' middle-class children, boys or white pupils. There is no place in the classroom for negative experiences. Advan-taged children must build on their advantage; the disadvantaged must be given full opportunity to match them by whatever means the teachers can make available.

Socialisation

An underlying reason for the differences between children before and during schooling is the process of socialisation that occurs in family, community and school (and continues through adult life), in which new members of society learn the culture – the values, attitudes, language and general life skills – that enables them to survive. It is an essential process of growth, but unlike physical growth social growth does not occur 'automatically'; it has to be learned from other human beings. And whilst there are aspects of common culture that virtually all members of society know and share, such as language, diet, religion and law, very many aspects are specific to groups within it. These subcultures, with recurring variations from the mainstream culture, can lead to widely varying life chances and prospects. And of course the sub-cultures in virtually all societies are those of social class, gender and race.

There are certainly many others, usually less permanent, such as the sub-cultures of a workplace, a club, a school, or even a school class. Human beings commonly put a great deal of effort into learning the appropriate culture patterns of social groups in which they find themselves or which they aspire to join. Unless they succeed they will never have the recognition of full membership and as a result will he confined to low, marginal roles and status or will even be 'outsiders'. All teachers know children who never quite make it in classroom acceptability and have seen the distress and anxiety such children experience.

The process of learning the culture or sub-culture is known as socialisation, and it is a process which can bring individuals together in behaviour and opportunity – or differentiate them.

For many years teachers have reinforced not only the learning of common culture but also the process of differential socialisation, helping middle-class children to become middle-class adults, boys to be men and girls to be women and, often, ethnic minority community children to occupy marginal adult roles. More recently, however, teachers have come to see more clearly that this process can lead not only to a kind of social stability but also to great injustice. It can lead to some children receiving status and power beyond their capabilities and others being denied the opportunity to use their capabilities fully. It is a fundamental assumption of this book that teachers wish to maximise the full capability of all their pupils. There are many reasons but three will suffice:

- justice to young people;

- the needs of all modern societies for developed human capability;

- the professional satisfaction of the teachers themselves.

Language

Let us now look at some aspects of socialisation particularly relevant to the teacher. One is language. We are in debt to Basil Bernstein for reminding us that there are two strikingly different kinds of language usage. His famous story (1961) of the two children on the bus is well known. There are many versions, but all involve two mothers and their equal concern for the safety of their respective children when the bus moves off. Mother A says, 'Sit down now, darling'. Her child says, 'Why?' and mother explains the risk of falling over in careful, detailed ways. After several more 'whys' mother is close to discussing centrifugal force. But when the bus actually moves she has to turn her request into a command. Mother B also asks her child to sit down, faced with 'Why?' she responds with 'I told you to sit down' and soon reaches 'If you don't sit down I'll knock your head off'.

In Bernstein's terminology, child A is being helped to acquire an elaborated code, with complex syntax and extended vocabulary so that eventually every subtlety of meaning can be expressed by words alone. It is a language that middle-class parents use in work and leisure, but also, more crucially, it is the language of the classroom, the textbook and the examination room. Without it success in mainstream education is difficult, even impossible. Child B is experiencing a restricted code of language, one with simple syntax and limited vocabulary. Full meaning requires the words to be augmented by gesture, expression or context. A good example is the building site, where workers may often employ the 'f' word for almost every adjectival or adverbial use, and yet achieve full communication. There are countless restricted codes; almost every permanent social group has its own. Most families have their own version and their use plays an important role in family bonding.

Yet teachers' preferences for elaborated codes, though understandable and largely necessary, should not lead them into the easy belief that these are always superior to restricted codes. Many films and novels have shown that restricted codes can convey, with non-verbal augmentation, a full range of subtle meanings.

Labov made the point clearly in his study (1969) of New York children. He showed that many had been identified by their teachers as being virtually without language capability and that test results confirmed this view. Such children were seen by teachers as virtually ineducable and their schooling had little prospect. The children responded with low motivation, low attendance and low co-operation with their teachers. Yet when Labov mixed with the children out of school he found that in their language they were able to conduct extended discussions and arguments involving complex issues of sport, popular music, community relationships, often much more demanding than the verbal reasoning required of them in the classroom. Yet sadly this capability remained unrecognised in their schooling and its assessment. It does not take many comments such as 'You cannot use that language in the classroom' to turn children into non-verbal members of the class. This point was recognised in the recommendations for the National Curriculum made by the Working Group on English, which urged teachers not to be over-insistent on the use of standard English at all times. Not surprisingly, the recommendation led to wide controversy.

Social Control
But the work of Bernstein and Labov alerts us not only to how language is used but to the significant consequences of its different uses. This is in issue of control. Child A on the bus was not only learning how to use elaborated language but also learning that by understanding and reason it is possible to control one's relationship with the environment and to use it to personal advantage. Child B was learning that personal behaviour is controlled by others; personal understanding is unnecessary, even irrelevant. The experiences point to different future lifestyles, lifestyles probably very similar to those of the children's parents: one based on ability to control situations and having power over others, the other based on being controlled by others. To use conceptual terms, the difference is between learning inner-directedness and other-directedness. Using our concept of socialisation, it could also be seen as the difference between two distinct patterns of anticipatory socialisation.

Most teachers recognise the importance of inner-directedness. It is after all, as we have seen, a crucial element of the teacher's own role. Similarly, all children need to feel they can control some parts of their own lives and enjoy their own 'space'. If children are precluded from, or feel unable to respond to the opportunities the teacher is offering them for personal space and control, then they are likely to set up alternative sub-cultures in which they can achieve it, as Labov's work clearly shows. For this reason teachers are often faced with the 'anti-group' in schools who find ways of 'counting for something' by adopting deviant, teacher-provoking ways of dress, hairstyle, language or behaviour which may be matched by delinquent and deviant behaviour out of school (e.g. Patrick, 1973).

Reinforcing Expectations

This discussion of language has focused on social class differences, though in the case of Labov's study the ethnic factor is also relevant since many of the children were black. Brandis and Henderson's study of primary schools (1974) found that, contrary to widespread expectations, parents from all social backgrounds were actively interested in teachers' views of their children and paid keen attention to them. However, there was a marked difference in the response of parents from different social groups. Middle-class parents faced with a less than enthusiastic commentary on their children sought to change the appraisal by giving extra assistance and support to the children and seeking to encourage the teachers to change their views. Working-class parents were equally concerned but tended to defer to the view of the teacher as the expert and to accept the situation. The inevitable consequence was a widening class gap as the differentiation was reaffirmed and built upon. Following the 1988 Education Reform Act and the 1992 Citizen's Charter, all parents in England and Wales will now receive regular information on their children's achievements in National Curriculum subjects. It will be vital for teachers to ensure that all parents are helped to respond effectively to the information they receive.

Many other writers have reaffirmed the class, gender and racial differentiation that is arbitrarily built up and that rapidly assumes permanent dimensions. Douglas (1964) documented how teachers' class-linked perceptions of children of similar ability led to wide variations in actual achievement through the period of primary education. Jackson and Marsden (1960) noted how schools handicapped parents who had little knowledge of the school curriculum and examinations by failing to recognise and remedy their need for better information, thereby diminishing their capability to support and guide their children's education or even to ask appropriate questions.

Delamont (1986), like many other writers, has shown how the expectations teachers hold about the education of girls are different from those they hold about boys and lead to familiar differences in subject choice. In every university the results are clearly to be seen on degree day: very few women receive degrees in engineering and technology, and not infrequently the lone woman engineering graduate receives a special round of applause, much as would be received by a severely disabled student! Sex stereotypes abound throughout education: 'Boys don't cry', 'Girls don't get dirty'. All readers will know these and many similar exhortations; they are indeed part of the culture of our society and as such are highly formative. We shall return to this theme in our chapter on the roles of children at school.

Eggleston *et al.* (1986) in a study of black young people and their parents showed how teachers underestimated and undervalued the capability and motivation of black children, even though in many cases the schools themselves had reliable evidence of it. In several of the schools the researchers investigated, able black children were assigned to lower-achieving groups; when challenged, teachers argued that this was done 'for social reasons'. At the heart of the 'reasons' were expectations that black children lacked the persistence, ambition and endurance to make it academically, assumptions that the research team demonstrated to be unfounded.

Eggleston and Sadler (1988) in a study of technical and vocational education found that schools were disappointed that black children and their parents were not more enthusiastic about the new opportunities on offer. But the research found that relatively little information was effectively reaching the parents: letters sent home with pupils were often not reaching the home, and even when they did, the letters' standard, formal English was often interpreted inaccurately or incompletely to the parents by the pupils. Conversely, the schools were receiving little or no information about the aspirations of parents and their support for education through such means as supplementary schooling or books and computers in the home. Thus erroneous assumptions about the lack of black parents' enthusiasm and support went unchallenged and once again formed the basis for decisions on examination entry, school reports and, thereby, life prospects. Smith and Tomlinson (1989) present clear evidence that, when schools break through these assumptions, the achievement of all pupils, white and black, can be enhanced and that the key variable is good teaching, not race. Much the same conclusion about social class is recorded by Mortimore *et al.* (1987):

> Those schools which were effective for one group tended to be effective for the other. Conversely, those which were ineffective for one group were also usually ineffective for the other. Our results show, therefore, that effective schools tend to 'jack up' the progress of all pupils, irrespective of their social class background, while ineffective schools will usually depress the progress of all pupils.

One of the main reasons for the perpetuation of the negative assumptions we have reviewed can be the needs of teachers! In a study by Sharp and Green (1975), 'Mrs Lyons' sees her pupils as:

> the products of largely unstable and uncultured backgrounds, with parents who are, in various combinations, irresponsible, incompetent, illiterate, clueless', uninterested and unappreciative of education, and who, as a result, fail to prepare their children adequately for the experiences they will be offered in school.

> The parents, especially the mothers, tend to be spoken of very disparagingly. The mothers are perceived as generally immature and unable to cope, having too many young children either by accident or design whilst they are still too young. The teacher declares that many mothers go to work to help pay off rent arrears and electricity bills incurred through bad management. She castigates them for creating latchkey children and for frittering away their conscience money on toys and unsuitable clothes in an attempt to relieve 'their guilt' at neglecting them.

'Mrs Lyons' is illustrating a rationalisation often used by teachers: holding children's backgrounds to blame for low achievement in school. There are some situations where this may be true, but to see it as the end of the matter is to condemn children to the constraints of their backgrounds. And of course it may well be that some of the factors listed by 'Mrs Lyons' do not exist at all or, if they do, are not constraints!

At the heart of the issues raised in this chapter there is one issue: should education really make a significant difference to the experience of child, parent and teacher? Or should it simply transmit to each new generation the social distinctions of class, gender and race? Should it in fact be simply a process of social and cultural reproduction as Bourdieu (1973) has described? The contention of this chapter is that it should not and need not be; but unless teachers are constantly vigilant it will be. It is facile, misleading and generally untrue to say that middle-class parents value education more than working-class parents, to say that the education of boys is seen to matter more than that of girls, or to say that black parents have lower understanding and expectation of education than white parents. On close examination, these assumptions turn out to be false; most of the evidence suggests that the differences are non-existent.

If education is to provide real equality of opportunity then all the understandings and misunderstandings we have listed in this chapter, and many more to which subsequent chapters draw attention, have to be re-examined. Such re-examination can best be begun in the classroom. To do it we need awareness of social and cultural background and a willingness not just to recognise but to understand and value alternative forms of knowledge, language and culture so that we can base the work of the classroom upon a positive analysis of all children.

Summary
This chapter has examined the role of the teacher in class, race and gender socialisation and indicated the crucial need to break through stereotypes of class, gender and race. If teachers cannot lead in this then many children have little hope of real achievement. If teachers succeed then they will have made education matter – identifying feasible and rewarding achievements for each child, and delivering them.

References
Bernstein, B. (1961) Social class and linguistic developments, in Floud, I., Halsey, A.A. and Anderson, C.A. (eds) *Education and Society.* Glencoe, Illinois: Free Press.

Bourdieu, P. (1973) Cultural reproduction and social reproduction, in Brown, R. (ed.) *Knowledge, Education and Cultural Change*. London: Tavistock.

Brandis, W. and Henderson, D. (1974) *Social Class, Language and Communication*. London: Routledge and Kegan Paul.

Delamont, S. (1986) *Sex Roles and the School*. London: Methuen.

Douglas, 1. W. B. (1964) *The Home and the School*. London: MacGibbon and Kee.

Eggleston, J. and Sadler, S. (1988) *The Participation of Ethnic Minority Pupils in TVEI*. Sheffield: The Training Agency.

Eggleston, I., Dunn, D. and Angali, M. (1986) *Education for Some*. Stoke-on-Trent: Trentham Books.

Jackson, B. and Marsden, D. (1960) *Education and the Working Class*. London: Routledge and Kegan Paul.

Labov, W. (1969) The logic of non-standard English, in Atlatis, I. (ed.) *School of Languages and Linguistics Monograph*, Series no. 22. Washington, DC: Georgetown University Press.

Mortimore, P. et a]. (1987) *School Matters: The Junior Years*. London: Open Books.

Patrick, 1. (1973) *A Glasgow Gang Observed*. London: Eyre Methuen.

Reid, 1. (1988) *The Sociology of Education*. London: Fontana.

Rutter, M. (1987) School effects on pupil progress, *Child Development* 34(1), pp. 1-9.

Sharp, R. and Green, A.G. (1975) *Education and Social Control*. London: Routledge and Kegan Paul.

Smith, D. I. and Tomlinson, S. (1989) *The School Effect*. London: Policy Studies Institute.

11

Staying on at School
The hidden curriculum of selection

Already in his seventies, John Eggleston obtained funding from Leverhulme to follow up some of the findings of the Eggleston Report (1986 – see chapter 8). In 2000, he published his findings with Trentham: Staying on at School. *This is the summary he placed in a Trentham journal,* Improving Schools *(Vol 3 No 2, 2000) which he edited for part of its life. He presents the main findings and, with his characteristic positivism and constructiveness, offers recommendations. His final one admonishes:*

 Remember that positive achievement, aspiration and self-esteem should always be enhanced and not diminished by teacher expectations and support, and uncontaminated by class, race or gender.

Of all the key decisions in education, the decision to stay on after minimum leaving age is probably the most important. It is at this point that the major distribution of career opportunities takes place. For most young people staying on means further or even initial accreditation. It is the point of entry to professional training, higher education and a more certain prospect of employment, higher earning, professional status and enhanced and desired life style.

But for those who leave at minimum leaving age a diminution of prospects, though not inescapable, becomes probable. They are more likely to lead to lower status occupations, lower pay, higher rates of initial and long term unemployment and a generally less favourable set of life chances.

Two opposing perspectives have dominated educational provision in most developed and developing countries in the past half century – and both have had profound effects on staying on. One, much favoured by economists, is that the enhancement of the education of an ever increasing segment of the labour market will deliver ever more marketable capabilities and favour both the economic development and growth in gross national product of the economy. The other, favoured by social scientists, is that social reproduction is endemic in most areas of society; that covert and overt processes tend to preserve the distribution of class, status and power from generation to generation and, without interventionist strategies, are therefore subversive to any labour market driven educational initiatives that threaten to modify this transmission.

For almost the same period the incidence of staying on after minimum school leaving age in modern compulsory education systems has been a crucial indicator of the interplay and efficacy of these two competing theories. It is and will remain a benchmark for successive British governments' dominant enthusiasm to prioritise educational achievement designed to produce a more educated and more economically effective labour force which, among other goals, seeks to eliminate poverty. Much of the enhanced education budget is focused on post-16 schooling, alternative post-16 examinations schemes such as NVQs and alternative A-levels, and the rapid expansion of the further education system. This political enthusiasm, broadly shared by most current governments across the world, can, in Britain, be dated back to the *Early Leaving Report* in 1954 and the ensuing Crowther Report 16-18 of 1959. In North America similar initiatives date from the 'Sputnik'-induced fears of educational inadequacy.

An associated but weaker long-term movement has been the furtherance of equality of opportunity across class, race and gender. Again, staying on decisions are a crucial indicator of the success or failure of this movement and here again the initiative has political roots (Eggleston, 1985). However, the political commitment is often weak and at best uneven, tending to rise after events such as the murder of

Stephen Lawrence in 1993 and the subsequent inquiry report (Macpherson, 1999) which aroused public concern, and quickly fade thereafter. Whilst enhanced equality of opportunity is an unreliable instrument of economic development, economic development is an equally unreliable means of enhancing social equality.

A broad spectrum of sociological analyses has pointed out the reasons. Full equality of educational achievement opens up the opportunity to exercise power to groups and categories that did not previously exercise it, so threatening the position of those who did. Both perspectives present significant challenge to existing social systems and pose a dilemma for governments who seek economic development in a largely unchanged social structure – a paradox and so unachievable. Bourdieu (1972) has made it clear in his analysis of social reproduction that cultural and economic socialisation are inseparable; changing one inevitably changes the other. But the general preference of all major political parties is to be able to initiate and steer social change instead of responding to it and this is almost certainly a major factor in the slowness of successive governmental initiatives to raise educational achievement.

This research attempts to throw light on the working of both perspectives by exploring the views of senior school students and their teachers about staying on at the point of minimum school leaving age. The interviews and questionnaires examined a number of key areas which included:

- The extent to which students approaching school leaving age are persuaded, by economic arguments in favour of staying on, to achieve more marketable accreditation

- Is the advice of teachers reinforcing economic arguments for staying on?

- The extent to which traditionally low aspiring group members (black, working class and for some subject areas, girls) are aspiring higher

- The attraction of new 'alternative academic' qualifications vis-a-vis 'traditional academic' paths and whether this response cuts across traditional class, gender and ethnic patterns

- Are schools facilitating or discouraging participation in further education by some or all of their students?

The detailed study of a small sample of schools was preceded by discussions held with senior staff and administrators in secondary schools throughout England.

The responses of the students and teachers

The overriding response of the teachers surveyed was that extended education is valuable and that staying on at school is the best way to get more of it. It was seen as enhancing life chances, keeping options open and as unquestionably beneficial for students' careers. And if students were not yet quite ready to appreciate this, staying on offered just the supportive environment needed to bring them to their senses. When asked if there were any circumstances in which students would be strongly advised not to stay on, almost all teachers replied that, in principle, there were virtually no such circumstances.

But underlying this enthusiasm was another – school self interest. Schools wanted quality staying on – in school. Motivated, able students were courted for their tonic effect on numbers and results. They and their parents formed a classic captive market and the hard sell was unmistakable. Further education was not presented as an option – indeed in many schools, as the Association of Colleges (1999) has reported, information on further education was regularly withheld.

There was little doubt that students had taken delivery of the schools' strong and unambiguous message carried in comments such as 'don't be stupid enough to leave at 16', 'don't let anybody persuade you to change your mind'. These views were strongly held by boys and girls from a wide range of ethnic majority and minority backgrounds in a selection of representative schools. The message was strongly influenced by prevailing economic attitudes. Typical reasons were: 'higher qualifications are a way of shining above the crowd', 'there's nothing out there if you don't'. Many students expressed it simply: 'I'll get a better job if I stay on', or even in a single word – 'money'.

There was also plenty of evidence that teachers were successfully embracing the traditional link between ambition and deferred.

gratification. Student responses included: 'I want to do all the hard work now and relax later', 'I want to make education the first thing I do before settling down', or as one student, perhaps with un-intended perception, put it: 'it will make me more intelligent'. But there was also an impressive air of self confidence among many res-pondents. As one British Caribbean girl said, 'I can do anything I put my mind to'. Often this was mixed with sharp awareness: 'even if I stay on and get good marks it doesn't necessarily mean I will get a good job' was how one British Asian boy summed things up.

However, students were also aware of their schools' economic motives and many commented on the advantages their schools would enjoy if they stayed on – what it would bring in resources, staffing and salaries, not to mention the enhancement of prestige and reputation. Many students expressed feelings of being manipulated – 'teachers talked about nothing else'. Some saw career counselling as an unambiguous pressure to stay on at school, and one British Caribbean girl said simply: 'they want to get bums on seats'. Some even saw a kind of teacher bribery: 'if enough of us stay on they have promised to set up the new media studies course we have been asking for', or 'they have promised to be more attentive and give us more freedom in the VIth form'.

With few exceptions, schools got what they wanted – a post-16 group of committed students, working for predominantly academic examinations and well supported by their homes. Overall this accounted for less than half of the 16+ age group – though the pro-portion varied predictably with the catchment areas. In the process virtually all the alienated, the trouble makers, the unmotivated and the low achievers quickly disappeared.

In an era of strong enthusiasm for economic egalitarianism how does this socio/academic selection persist? Why is it that in the schools surveyed less than half of the pupils actually stayed on and why did the social class system prevail, in that a majority of the students of middle class origin stayed on and only small groups, albeit growing, of working class students did so?

The answer lies in a two-fold process using instruments of guidance and curriculum. Let us take guidance first. Although teachers were initially unanimous in their enthusiasm to offer staying on for all students, the enthusiasm faded when they were confronted with the question 'What would lead you to discourage a student from staying on at 16?' The list turned out to be a long one. Pregnancy topped it as an almost total eliminator, but there were a number of other more directly school-related factors, including truancy, non-compliance, disinterest, non-motivation, and a range of other unwanted behaviours, some of which had already led to exclusion or expulsion. British African-Caribbean boys were more frequently seen as occupying some of these categories, although teachers were quick to emphasise that 'they were not the only ones'. But a social class linkage if not an ethnic linkage with undesirability was unmistakable; obliquely expressed as 'what can you expect from a family like that?'

The unwanted few were in no doubt of their identity – 'those teachers want me out of here as soon as they can get me' (British Asian girl ambitious to be a doctor). 'Staying on! – they are trying to expel me now' (white boy who wanted to stay on with a view to reading Law). Conversely, the chosen received very clear signals. 'They would like me to stay on because 1 am a very hard worker', or simply, 'they think I am clever'.

The invisibility of further education colleges

But the message was not only to 'stay on' but to 'stay here'. Little guidance on further education was on offer, still less any preparation for it. For most schools, with or without a VIth form, further education was another world and even if the teachers did know about it, it was not seen as part of their job to tell their students. Hostile competition accurately sums up how many teachers perceived matters: The Association of Colleges (1999) reports that many colleges no longer ask schools for references because the heads then interview the students and browbeat them to stay at school, also that many schools refuse to supply colleges with names of school leavers and even misinform students that college courses are full.

At a time when there is intense governmental enthusiasm and emphasis on further education in England and Wales (currently with over 3.5 million students and a £3.3 billion pounds annual expenditure, much of it specifically designed to rescue the talent being lost through leaving at 16+) the failure of schools to prepare or support students for further education is surprising.

The fault line at 16+ is so fundamental that most students who enter further education have to be recruited to education all over again at formidable cost and, often, with only modest success. This was evident in the way that students discovered further education by alternative, non-school means. Most common were the widely available college brochures – glossy and expensively produced – augmented by local radio, bus and poster advertising and open days.

For many students the college message was reinforced by the social groups in which school and college students mixed out of school. Indeed the mixed age groupings were seen as one of the main attractions of further education. In one school where the staying on message was particularly strongly emphasised, some 80% of the 15 year old group expressed a desire to go to college rather than stay at school. The ensuing reality was difficult to assess but clearly otherwise. Estimates suggested that, overall, just under 50% eventually stayed on at school and, at most, a quarter signed up for further education on or soon after leaving.

Curriculum choices

School guidance factors were crucially reinforced by curriculum factors. Most teachers agreed that 'traditional' academic subjects were the best vehicle for most post-16 study. The old advice that success in English, maths and science, preferably confirmed by good A-level grades, will really prove your capability', was now augmented by the argument that these subjects were much more marketable for career or university access. It was advice that accorded with the views of middle class parents; as one, British-Asian, girl put it, 'my mum always advises me to do the hard subjects as they are more worthwhile'. Far less in accord were the views of the working class parents who saw an A-level as an A-level, so that if their children wanted to take media studies or design and technology, 'well, why not?' In most schools there was little consideration of alternatives such as GNVQ and Modern Apprenticeship schemes. Even though in a few cases schools had entered some students for Part 1 GNVQ, their teachers were prepared to argue that their success in Part 1 was a good omen for at least a modest attempt at some A-levels even if not mainstream ones.

For the students a main attraction of further education, apart from the promise of freedom, was the curriculum. Media studies, business studies, child care, leisure studies, pre-nursing courses – all these were frequently frowned upon by their teachers at school. 'I want to take IT and graphic design but the school wants me to do A-level French and history' was one typical comment, from an African origin boy. It was not only the range of subjects on offer in further education but also the prospect of hands on, practical experience as opposed to the text dominance of the schools' offering that attracted them. Few schools showed enthusiasm for work experience. The result was a conflict for many students of all backgrounds and abilities. Yet although there were examples of 'deviant' decisions the overall outcome was consistent: pupils from the upper end of the social class spectrum tended to stay on at school to study 'traditional' A-level subjects and practice the deferred gratification emphasised by both parents and teachers, whilst those at the lower end of the spectrum tended to find their own way into further education, employment or simply disappear from the scene.

Almost thirty years ago Bernstein's research (1971) showed how the ways in which schools make curriculum available to students is one of the main determinants of life chances. Despite three decades in which his work has been expounded in countless teacher training courses, Open University degree programmes for teachers and in in-service programmes, little if anything has changed.

Class and Ethnicity

There was evidence of the attempts by some families and their students to cross the 'class allocation system'. These were largely confined to students from ethnic minority backgrounds – especially those from the Indian subcontinent – who displayed determined attempts to 'make it', usually using a school influenced strategy. 'My mother said go into medicine for money and social status. So 1 have decided to be a doctor. My ancestors were not of high caste and I needed to prove my worth to myself and to others'. There was also a strong hint of pressure from some Asian parents – 'no living in my house if you don't want to make the most of yourself'.

Conversely the school with a majority of students of white working class origin displayed the highest proportion of students wanting to leave at 16. They made frequent comments such as, 'it's a waste of time', 'boring', 'I don't achieve nothing at school', 'they hate me and I hate them', 'I want to get a job and earn some real money'. Many of the students wrote 'White British' on their questionnaires where asked for their ethnic identifications, sometimes augmented, for good measure, with a Union flag.

Recommendations for practice

Throughout the study the pervasive influence of teachers was greatly in evidence and usually, although not always, explicitly acknowledged by students. However peer group influences were of great significance in determining not only staying on but also the educational programmes students selected. The peer group was particularly influential in its combination of realism and idealism regarding career choice. This co-existed with high career and salary ambitions and a life style in which hi-tech leisure played an important part. Idealism and economic success were seldom seen to be incompatible.

Despite the growing abundance of new accreditation opportunities and training programmes, young people showed a keen ability to stay in touch with new developments and also be aware of the traditional hierarchy of examinations, institutions, programmes and schemes. Often they were more aware than the teachers of the negotiable market value of the qualifications offered and the status of the alumni of different colleges and universities. Young people were commonly able to display extensive knowledge of the distinctions between the old universities and the new. In particular they were well aware that high achievement in low status qualifications and subjects might well be of less value than modest achievement in high status qualifications and subjects. They were also able to compare the 'pay offs' of non-vocational as against vocational degrees.

Teachers sometimes failed to take account of how widely such understandings are discussed on TV and in the media generally. As a result they not infrequently undervalued the realistic ambitions of young people, particularly those in schools where high aspirations, career and post-school education are not well established. A desire not to let young people be hurt by over ambition led some teachers to inhibit feasible aspirations – particularly in the case of girls and black students. Certainly there was a high correlation between success and positive self-image in virtually all the schools surveyed. However there was plenty of indication in the responses of both students and teachers that long established variables of class, gender and race have by no means disappeared, though some are now covert rather than overt. Sewell (1997), in an important book published towards the completion of the project, outlined a range of effective strategies that teachers and students can use together to help achieve positive behaviour in schools. In work with young black males, Sewell reaffirmed that the school variable rather than the race variable was often the key determinant of academic success.

The present report leads to the following recommendations, addressed to teachers and careers advisers:

- Do not restrict information on post-16 opportunities for your students but help them instead to make fully informed choices. If they decide to stay on at school let it be in the full knowledge of what the school can offer as compared with other educational institutions, notably further education. Be sure that your advice is determined by the students' needs rather than those of the schools and teachers. If you have a conflict of interest, explain and discuss it. Students will probably have recognised this already and will respect your openness. If you are a further education tutor the same considerations should govern your behaviour.

- Listen to students' own appraisal of staying on and the programmes to which it might lead; their awareness is often illuminating and highly impressive.

- Consider carefully your own concepts of high status knowledge and its implications for young people. Even if they still appear to be valid, does the the narrowness of your conception needlessly restrict the numbers who can benefit? By redefining high status knowledge – or enhancing access – could you enhance the future of more young people?

- Be slow to dismiss any ambitions that appear to you to be unrealistic. Many students are successfully challenging restrictive stereotypes, but the culture of the school may still be an impediment. Take particular care that your advice and judgement is based on a true appraisal of students' ability and capability, uncontaminated by assumptions based on class, gender or race.

• Be attuned to career profiles portrayed in the media as much as to 'official' careers literature and be prepared to discuss them objectively and in a contemporary time frame. The 'soaps' provide rich examples; do not ignore their powerful influence.

• Be as familiar with the business and professional pages as you are with news pages of both broadsheet and tabloid newspapers. In particular, study the appointments supplements; the advice is often more up to date than most career manuals.

• Help young people to realise that the deferred gratification commonly associated with prolonged study is not total and draw their attention to some of the pleasures and immediate gratifications of student life. Invite a broad spectrum of recent leavers back to school to talk with the 15+ cohort, including, if they and you can handle it, some of the less successful.

• Don't underplay the satisfactions of extended study for its own sake; young people are often glad to be so reminded as a reinforcement of their own self-concept of ability.

• Money is important to young people – perhaps never more than now. Help them to become financially competent – many higher and further education students fail to complete their courses simply because they cannot cope with their finances.

• Never underestimate the idealism of young people. This research revealed that social service, welfare, help for the disabled, conservation and environmentalism are often major motivations which surmount all others. But remember that this idealism is not incompatible with well paid, high status careers or the extended educational prospects needed to achieve them.

Remember that positive achievement, aspiration and self-esteem should always be enhanced and not diminished by teacher expectations and support, and uncontaminated by class, race or gender. It can and should flourish fully in any educational establishment – in schools, further and higher education. Sadly, this still requires a fundamental change in the professional approach of many teachers and many students. Without it, aspirations for equal opportunity and a maximally trained labour force will not be fulfilled.

Conclusion

Despite many inconsistencies the outcome of this research suggests that, overall, little has changed since the *Early Leaving Report* of the 1950s, which displayed a social gradient that was remarkably similar to the infant mortality figures of the period. Yet though infant mortality, like early leaving, has been reduced dramatically in the ensuing half century, the social gradient seems also little changed. The huge expansion in educational opportunity from preschool to higher education and, most notably, in further education has resulted in greatly increased participation. But even though the volume and range of educational opportunity is now vast, at 16+ very little progress has been made in ensuring a fuller match between students' capability, opportunity and achievement regardless of social class and much of that progress has been among families with roots in the Indian sub-continent.

We have come to realise that structural equality of provision does not deliver social equality of opportunity. The prevailing tradition of the schools, the gulf between schools and further education and the substantially unchallenged social class system regularly reinforced by peer and street culture makes sure that it does not. Transfer at 16+ urgently needs the careful study we are now giving, belatedly, to transfer at 11+.

References

Association of Colleges (1999) *School-College Competition for 16 year old Pupils*, London: AOC

Bernstein, B. (1971) 'On the Classification and Framing of Educational Knowledge' in Young, M. ed, *Knowledge and Control*, London: Collier-Macmillan.

Bourdieu, P. (1972) *La Reproduction*. Paris: Editions de Minuit

Crowther Report (1959) *16-18*, London: HMSO

Eggleston, J., Dunn, D., and Anjali, M. (1986) *Education for Some*, Stoke on Trent: Trentham

Macpherson Report (1999) *The Stephen Lawrence Inquiry*, London: HMSO

Sewell, T. (1997) *Black Masculinities and Schooling,* Stoke on Trent: Trentham

A fuller version of this report, *Staying on at School* is published by Trentham Books.

12

What is Design and Technology?

Teaching Design and Technology, 3rd ed, 2001

John Eggleston died in December 2001, a year in which he produced two books. Teaching and Learning Design Technology: a guide to its recent research and its applications (Continuum) *is an edited collection of the new research and practice in the field, much of it led by Richard Tufnell and the team at Middlesex University, where John was Visiting Professor. His inaugural lecture in 1999 was an ambitious linking of his major concerns in the value of education in shaping children's future lives, the value of making things and particularly working out how to, and the links to the upcoming new curriculum subject, Citizenship Education.*

In 2001, the Open University published the third edition of his Teaching Design and Technology. *This had become the standard text for how to teach the subject, but the subject was again changing in response to government directives. John had complained gently that this third revision needed to be a virtual rewrite. So that is what he did.*

The brief extract from the introductory chapter and the fuller extract from chapter 2 provide a fitting end to this collection. It illustrates John's broad vision of Design and Technology as informing all aspects of modern life and it reflects his abiding vision of education as inclusive and holistic – a vision for today.

The last word, taken from this chapter, comes from John:

Every citizen needs to be familiar with a wide range of technology in order to have sufficient understanding and capacity to live effectively in modern society... these technologies determine the quality of life and range of opportunity of every citizen.

Design and Technology is one of the fastest growth areas of the contemporary school curriculum. Government ministers and leading industrialists and educators vie with each other to emphasise the crucial role for Design and Technology in the future, even for the survival of the national economy and for the long-term employment prospects for individuals. In Britain the Technical and Vocational Education Initiative (TVEI) began in 1986; the Training Agency (formerly the Manpower Services Commission) pumped millions of pounds into developing technological education in schools; millions more followed in the national extension. By the mid 1980s, in some of the rural areas of England and Wales, British Schools Technology (BST) buses had become more frequent sights than passenger service buses. Meanwhile new GCSE syllabuses had rapidly translated the remnants of Craft, Design and Technology (CDT), Home Economics, and associated subjects into the new subject area. The National Curriculum with its incorporation of Technology as a foundation subject is speeding the changes still more rapidly in secondary and primary schools. Throughout the nation, there is evidence that, in primary and secondary schools, the new programmes are burgeoning.

What survived all of this into the National Curriculum was Design Technology. It is the one conspicuous innovation in the Education Reform Act 1988, and it draws together elements from previous domains with an assurance that neither integrated science nor integrated humanities come near to attaining. The continued enthusiasm for a technologically literate nation has been accelerated by the Labour Government's prioritisation of education, and the growth curve has become even steeper.

Yet although this book is about one of the newest areas in the school curriculum it is also one of the oldest – the ways in which students in schools work with materials – with wood and clay, metal and concrete, paper and plastics, and with food and fabrics. But of course Design and Technology is not only about the manipulation of materials but also about the complex series of judgements, about the needs that give rise to that manipulation and the responses to such needs. So the evidence of Design and Technology activity is not only manipulation but also drawing, writing, talking and modelling.

The range of work is vast; the history of many of the activities is as old as humanity itself. Yet only recently have we begun to realise the full potential of this area of the school curriculum. Not only have we discovered a wide range of new and previously unused processes and materials, but we have also rediscovered the intellectual as well as the practical learning that can take place in work with materials. Above all we have realised more fundamentally than ever before that, in a modern society, human capacity to use and to modify the environment is critically determined by capacity to understand, plan and utilise resources of three-dimensional materials. Their availability and well-designed manipulation are as essential to the activities of an advanced industrial economy as they have been to those of any previous social system. Their importance in every phase of human pursuit from the most basic to the most esoteric is self-evident; their importance in the capacity of humans to express themselves has probably never been so great. And as the scarcity of natural resources intensifies and the cost of materials produced from them rises, the argument for work in the school that enhances thought and discrimination in their use becomes ever more compelling.

CHAPTER 2
WHAT IS DESIGN AND TECHNOLOGY?

This chapter explores the distinct yet linked natures of both Technology and Design and considers why both are essential components of the school curriculum. Examples of work in schools are offered and the implications for adult roles in work, home, leisure and community are discussed.

Design and Technology is now a compulsory subject from the age of 5 for all children in State schools in England, for most up to 16 years, and in Wales up to 14 years. Moreover, there is every sign that most independent schools are following suit. Yet the precise identity of this relatively new subject is still unclear to many teachers – either through total or partial unfamiliarity with it in their professional training or in their experience to date. This chapter attempts to remedy this deficiency for teachers and, hopefully, enable them to know and to explain the nature of their subject to even more bewildered parents, employers and pupils.

Design and Technology is unique in the school curriculum. It is the one subject directly concerned with the individual's capacity to design and make, to solve problems with the use of materials and to understand the significance of Technology.

It is easiest to begin to define Design and Technology by reference to the National Curriculum. Essentially this was defined in the Attainment Targets in the original Order. [cites DfEE/QCA 1999] the Working Group Report (DES, 1989). ...

But few schools have presented the curriculum in a way that fully incorporates it or even identifies the true nature of Design and Technology. In some schools Technology and Design are still seen as discrete areas of activity – taking place in workshops and studios, respectively, with a dominantly practical nature and largely unrelated to the other subjects in the curriculum.

The incidence of Technology issues across the curriculum was interestingly displayed in an early APU study undertaken at the then Trent Polytechnic. It divided Technology into three components, value judgements, knowledge and skills and explored where they occurred in the curriculum. The exercise threw up some interesting illumination – for instance the considerable attention being paid by Religious Education classes to the technology of warfare and its human and social consequences (the study was undertaken during the Falklands War and could almost certainly have been replicated during the Gulf War or the Kosovo conflict). The importance of values in any full study of Technology has been emphasised by Ruth Conway (1990):

> ... technology education is not just an instrumental activity, giving pupils the knowledge, skills and resources to be able to make things, but should be encouraging pupils to harness their creative abilities towards goals that they have consciously chosen and evaluated, with growing sensitivity to the needs of other people and the environment, and responsible decision-making.

The nature of technology

The problems of identity of both Technology and Design in the curriculum are exacerbated by the long and complex history of both areas in society at large. Technology has played a major role in the development of civilisation – in the long path from primitive, nomadic, minimal livelihood to the opportunities of sophisticated modern society. Yet until comparatively recent times the technologists who created the cathedrals and all other enduring buildings, the roads and highways, the canals, the coaches and other vehicles, the heating and lighting systems and much more, have been largely invisible. Usually only the patrons were identified. Only in the eighteenth and nineteenth centuries did things begin to change spectacularly with the achievements of some of the technologists – Wren, Brunel, Arkwright and others. It was only in the nineteenth and twentieth centuries that the great national institutions were founded: The Institution of Mechanical Engineers, The Institution of Chemical Engineers, The Royal Institute of British Architects, The Institute of Chartered Accountants – all these were nineteenth- or twentieth-century inventions. Indeed, it is only in very recent times that accountants and bankers have been recognised as technologists in any regular way. Only in the mid-twentieth century has the accreditation of Technology and associated programmes of study been fully formulated for virtually all branches of technology.

Elsewhere Technology was being delivered by craftsmen and women or people who, in the twentieth century, have become more generally known as 'technicians'. The immense social significance of the distinction between the terms technologist and technician cannot be overemphasised. The term 'technician' came to cover the full range of people who did technology – who made things work and continued to make them work. But their status was inferior; they worked to the orders of their patrons, clients, employers or managers who were not required to have any of the requisite practical technical knowledge or capability. The establishment of the role of professional technologist such as the engineers, architects, town planners and financiers reinforced rather than diminished this distinction. In their training and in their professional work there was no need for them to lay bricks or saw timber. No mechanical engineer needed to be able to machine metal or assemble machinery. Essentially their role was cerebral rather than manual.

The segregation of technical education followed the segregation of the occupational structure. The most able children in the schools – selected by their achievements in academic subjects (notably Science, Literature and Language) – proceeded to higher education and to follow professional and managerial courses. The less able left school at minimum learning age and, unqualified, became apprentices or some form of on-the-job trainees, perhaps to achieve technician status. For some, training became available in Technical Schools and Vocational Classes. We have already considered, in Chapter 1, the low status of these courses and the low status prospects of those who followed them. Essentially they were seen as avenues for less able pupils to become occupationally useful.

Technology education in the National Curriculum marks an attempt to override such old distinctions and especially to break out of the low status of technical education and to bring technological education from higher education into the schools. It is also an attempt to demonstrate that technology is an appropriate and important subject for the education of all children including the most able. Furthermore, it is making the point that not only technicians but also technologists and indeed all citizens need to be able to understand, develop and handle technology in all its aspects. If it succeeds it may achieve a major goal – to break down the status barriers which have so long impeded the economic development of England and Wales and many other Western countries – the low status of actually making things in a system controlled by those who do not. The spectacular success of Japanese manufacturing industry where, culturally, these divisions do not exist offers a justification of the need for such a change. But to achieve these goals it is vital that Technology in schools does not suffer the same pitfalls and devalue sound practical capability. The danger of turning technology into a subject where realisation is only the making of drawings and models is considerable.

But of course Technology education is not only about occupation. Every citizen needs to be familiar with a wide range of technology in order to have sufficient understanding and capacity to live effectively in modern society: electrical, financial, child-rearing and architectural technology – these and many more technologies determine the quality of life and range of opportunity of every citizen. Individuals must not only be able to involve themselves in technology but also be able to enter into effective dialogue with the professional technologists who every day are making key decisions about their lives and welfare. Just as the technologists need to be able to think and make, so do the non-technologists need to be able to make and think about technology.

The nature of design

The nature and status of design is at least as complex as that of technology. Archer (1973) wrote:

> Design is that area of human experience, skill and knowledge which is concerned with man's ability to mould his environment, to suit his material and spiritual needs.... There is a sufficient body of knowledge for this area called 'design' to be developed to a level which will merit scholarly regard for the future.

At the heart of the matter is the design process. This is the process of problem-solving which begins with a detailed preliminary identification of a problem and a diagnosis of needs that have to be met by a solution, and goes through a series of stages in which various solutions are conceived, explored and evaluated until an optimum answer is found that appears to satisfy the necessary criteria as fully as possible within the limits and opportunities available. The design process at its most complete is one that can be used to describe, to analyse and hopefully to improve every aspect of human activity and especially those human activities that lead to end products and services. Jones (1970) put it effectively when he said 'the effect of designing is to initiate change in man-made things'. But of fundamental importance in the concept of design is rationality. The design process above all else is one of rational, logical analysis. Jones emphasised this strongly, commenting that the picture of the designer is

> very much that of a human computer, a person who operates only on the information that is fed to him and who follows through a planned sequence of analytical, synthetic and evaluative steps and cycles until he recognises the best of all possible solutions.

Defined in this way, the concept of design was given its most powerful impact in the work of the Bauhaus, an industrial arts school in
pre-war Germany. Here, in close association with artists and thinkers
such as Gropius, Kandinsky and Klee, there developed a new and
powerful movement to explore fundamentally and rigorously the
process of design as a human activity.

Until the time of the Bauhaus the form of hand and machine-made
objects had normally been achieved by a combination of tradition,
expediency and chance. Design was commonly a unilateral activity
in which the requirements of one participant tended to predominate
and often to monopolise the specifications. Thus, the craftsman
alone could impose considerations of skill or availability of material;
the engineer alone could impose technological requirements; the
client alone could impose considerations of taste or finance. Not infrequently the result of such 'designing' was brilliantly successful –
but only occasionally and incompletely was it rational. The Bauhaus
set out to change all this. Students were encouraged to study the process of design in a way that was both total and detailed. The results
were of central importance; the new wave of industrial design that
began in the inter-war years revolutionised the chaos of design in a
multitude of manufactured products. To some extent, many of the
most famous industrial products of the mid-twentieth century and
their familiar logos owe some debt to the influence of the Bauhaus
including the Braun food mixer, the Volkswagen 'Beetle' and the
Olivetti typewriter.

In the art colleges of Europe and the United States, the Bauhaus influence was widespread. It did much to develop among students a
concern for purity and simplicity of form and an appreciation of
properties of materials, of colour and texture, that by comparison
with what had gone before appeared to be austere, even chaste. To a
great extent it was responsible for the concept of the foundation
course, still almost a mandatory part of most art school courses, in
which students undertake fundamental explorations of the nature
and the property of materials. But it is easy for any new movement
to become obsessional, and the rationality and purity of the design
movement was no exception.

Like any system of ideas, the design process was certainly guilty of over-sophistication, rigidity and abuse. A particular problem was that design came to be an exercise for designers. It was an exercise in which, by virtue of their knowledge of the rules, they came to hold power and control, and in which all other participants, often including the client, came to be imprisoned in the designer's ethic. More recently, we have come to realise yet again that there are many participants in the process of design and that not all of them act in a wholly rational way or even accept the 'rationale' of the designer.

In the closing years of the twentieth century there has been a sharp reaction to the design movement, as individuals have sought to re-impose their feeling and individuality on designed products of all kinds led, in the UK, by Prince Charles in his commentary on modern architecture. At a personal level, this is perhaps most strikingly to be seen in the world of leisure where, for example, motor car owners have sought, with much energy, to make their mass-produced cars distinctive from those of other people, and thereby in some way to express their own self-image and lifestyle. It is only necessary to purchase a copy of a popular car magazine or to read the works of Tom Wolfe to see how widespread and effective such a movement is. It is a movement that will sometimes lead individuals to apparently extreme lengths to satisfy its aims. Fashions in leisure equipment such as motor cycles, clothing, mobile phones and music systems may be adopted not so much on technological criteria but on their potential for self-image, style and personal expression – as any parent of adolescents or even young children knows well.

[The chapter continues with a consideration of the design and technological process in the schools, harking back to the author's own Schools Council Project on Design and Craft Education in the 1970s. He works out the design and technology process in fine detail. First he suggests a project at Key Stage 4 by a group in a local school. He continues:]

Let us suppose that the school has a project that aims to involve its students more fully in the community in which they live, to give them the experience of responsibility, decision-making and participation in local affairs. Let us assume that the school is serving a large and somewhat underprivileged housing estate in an industrial city. As in many similar situations, the school is attempting to improve the facilities of the neighbourhood as part of the project. An often needed facility is equipment for younger children to play with in their leisure time. The designing of such equipment would almost certainly be seen to be a major responsibility of the Design and Technology department of the school.

[How, he asks, would this be done? In the following five pages, he examines every aspect of the process. From this he extrapolates the characteristics of the design process:]

1   Students have had the opportunity to experience and participate actively in an inventive and creative process in which new ideas can be developed and old ones modified. In these processes they have also had the experience of responsible decision-making in which not only have their ideas been used, but the responsibility for this use and its consequences on the lives of others has been unmistakably their own.

2   Students have come to see, in a way often impeded by traditional school curricula, the interplay of knowledge and understanding, how the work of one 'subject' complements and augments that of another, and how few, if any, problems can be solved with a narrow subject orientation. Many ideas, many resources, and many materials are called for in the solution of almost all human problems.

3   Students have become aware of the social context of human behaviour. This example, like almost all other manifestations of the Design and Technology process, made it clear that decision-making cannot be undertaken in isolation. The resources and needs of the clients, the parents, the community as a whole, even the wider society, have to be taken into account, and solutions have to satisfy all these participants if they are to be, in any real sense, an adequate response to a problem.

4   The long-standing concerns for skilled performance and the integrity and honesty of work are all honoured in a project of this kind. Skilled work is essential if the equipment constructed is to serve the purpose for which it was intended, and the safety of its users to be ensured. In addition other materials such as

concrete, requiring different but still unmistakably skilled handling, may also be introduced. The difference from many previous craft activities is that here skill is being used in a meaningful rather than an artificial context: its acquisition and its employment can be justified to even the most cynical parent or the least sympathetic teacher,

5   Above all, the Design and Technology process provides a tool of enquiry which, once experienced, will probably have a wide general applicability in the adult life likely to be experienced by the students, it is a process that will link rather than isolate them from the economic and social aspects of adult community in which they live.

[And he goes on to argue the interweaving of technology and society:]

In the past we have spoken not only about workers but about artists, woodworkers, needleworkers and the like. But here we are talking about the generic roles that increasingly characterise modern society – such as home owners, sportsmen and women and amateur gardeners: designations that imply a wide-ranging use of ideas and materials. The integration that is central to the Design and Technology process – the integration of specialist skills in a social context – is also central to the roles of modern society.

But there is yet a further and possibly even more compelling characteristic of the Design and Technology education component of the school curriculum. It springs from the new realisation in modern societies on both sides of the Atlantic that the material environment, both public and private, is above all a product of countless individual decisions. For many years we were convinced that decisions about our material environment were best left to the experts. Accordingly, we trained small numbers of highly selected designers, town planners, town and country planning officers, landscape artists and the like, and believed that, with their training, these specialists would be able to make appropriate, wise decisions. All that then remained was to persuade the majority of people, largely through the experience of schooling, to respond to their wisdom. In the Design and Technology subjects in particular, we endeavoured to introduce the experts' decisions to our students and to encourage them to accept them. We took them to the Design Centre and other exhibitions of 'good design' and allowed them to see the products which they could and should use in their homes. We took them to see the exhibitions of the planning consultants for their city and taught them to respect the wise suggestions made for the development of their civic environment. In doing this we overlooked, as did many of the adherents of the Bauhaus (see above), the realisation that the environment is never wholly determined by the decision of planners or consultants, even though indeed their suggestions are at times adopted. It is determined far more by the way in which ordinary men and women use their environment. It is determined by what they plant and what they construct in their gardens, by the way in which they decorate and locate their caravans, by the way they use public facilities and by the way they decide to spend their money and their leisure. A leading consultant on urban planning conceded, after many years of successful and well-regarded public practice, that he has now found it necessary to take into account the fact that, regardless of almost every known control, ordinary people found ways of constructing sheds or out-houses in their back gardens. He announced that henceforth he would 'take cognisance' of this in the preparation of his schemes!

In such ways we have become aware that we are more likely to achieve 'good design' in our environment if we recognise the participatory nature of design processes. Nicholson (1972) went so far as to suggest in his 'theory of loose parts' that the more successfully that technologists and. designers create a 'non-participant environment', the more successfully will people attempt to participate and establish their individual presence in it, even to the extent of behaviour which is labelled as vandalism. The 'structural modifications' that take place in waiting rooms and public conveniences help to make Nicholson's point. Increasingly an education designed to inculcate respect, to put people into a 'received' environment, is gradually giving way to an education in which people are expected to participate in: decision-making processes concerning their environment. In doing so they become active rather than passive participants in a modern society.

Conclusion

The experience of Design and Technology education that has been described in this chapter is nothing less than a preparation for such a participative role, and it is argued that this constitutes the most sufficient justification for the new subjects identity of Design and Technology education. The task of subsequent chapters will be to identify more fully the practice of this essential preparation for adult life offered by Design and Technology education.

References

Archer, L. B. (1973) 'The need for design education', Paper presented to DES conference N805, Horn. castle. Mimeo. London: Royal College of Art.

Assessment of Performance Unit (APU) (1983) *Design and Technology Performance* (Trent Polytechnic Survey). London: DES.

Conway, R. (1990) 'Values in technology'. *Times Educational Supplement*, 28 September, p. 22.

Department for Education (1992) *Technology for Ages 5-16*. London: WE.

Department for Education (1995) *Design and Technology in the National Curriculum*. London: HMSO. Department for Education and Employment/ Qualifications and Curriculum Authority (1999) *Design and Technology, Key Stages 1-4*. London: QCA.

Department of Education and Science (1989) *Design and Technology for Ages 5-16 (Final Report of the Working Group on Design and Technology)*. London: HMSO.

Department of Education and Science (1990) *Technology in the National Curriculum*. London: HMSO.

De Sausmarez, M. (1964) *Basic Design: The Dynamics of Visual Form*. London: Studio Vista.

Design and Craft Education Project (1971) *Design for Today*. London: Edward Arnold.

Jones. J. C. (1970) *Design Methods and Technology: Seeds of Human Futures*. London: John Wiley.

Layton. D. (1992) Values of Design and Technology', in Bodgett-Meakise (ed.) *Make the Future Work*. London: Longman.

Martin, M. (1998) 'Support for exploring values issues'. *Data News,* January, 11.

National Curriculum Council (1993) *Technology Programmes of Study and Attainment Targets*. York: NCC.

Project Technology (1971) *Final Report*. London: Schools Council.

Siraj-Blatchford, J. (1996) *From Collective Design to Design Collective*. Nottingham: Education Now Books.

CURRICULUM VITAE

EMERITUS PROFESSOR
SAMUEL JOHN EGGLESTON

Qualifications: 1949 Teacher's Certificate
1955 Awarded Leverhuline Scholarship
1957 BSc (Econ) University of London,
London School of Economics, (Economics,
Sociology, Psychology)
1959 Academic Diploma m Education, University of
London
1965 MA University of London
1977 DLitt University of Keele

Honorary
Awards:
1969 Fellow of the College of Craft Education
1980 Fellow of the RoYal Society of Arts
1981 Fellow of the College of Preceptors (*Honoris*
Causas)
1994 D Univ Hon) Middlesex University
1999 D Ed (Hon) University of Sunderland
2001 Fellow of the City and Guilds of London Institute
1950-1960 Taught special and secondary schools
1960-63 Lecturer m Sociology of Education,
Loughborough College of Education
Part-time tutor, University of Nottingham,
Department of Extra Mural Studies (including
experimental industrial courses) and University of
Leicester, Department of Adult Education
1963-67 Lecturer. subsequently Senior Lecturer, in
Education, University of Leicester

1967-84 Professor of Education and Head of
Department of Education, University of Keele
1985-94 Professor of Education and Chairman of
Education, University of Warwick
1994- Emeritus Professor and Leverhulme Fellow,
University of Warwick
1994- Visiting Professor, University of Central England
1996-2000 Non-Medical Education and Training
Adviser N.H.S. Trent

Major External Activities in United Kingdom

Visiting Lecturer in main fields of personal academic interest in most
Universities, Colleges of Higher Education and Art, and most major
national and regional conferences in those fields.

Member of:

1968-1977	House of Commons Working Group on Education for the Eradication of Colour Prejudice
1970-74	Schools Council of England and Wales – Working Party on whole Curriculum
1973-77	United Kingdom Social Science Research Council, Educational Research Board
1976-80	Department of Education and Science Assessment of Performance Unit Co-ordinating Committee
1976-80	Research Committee, National Youth Bureau (Chairman)
1976-83	CNAA Art and Design Committee and In-service Education Board Chair of Visitation Committees for the Council in a number of Polytechnics and Colleges
1977-78	Chair, SSRC seminar on decision making in the classroom – Report Published 1979
1978-79	Chair, SSRC seminar on the relationship between research and educational policy and practice
1978-80	Schools Committee, Independent Broadcasting Authority

1978-83	Teacher Education Committee, Commission for Racial Equality
1980-89	Consultative Committee (plus a range of working parties) Assessment of Performance Unit, Department of Education and Science
1980-83	Department of Education and Science Research Consultancy
1981-83	Cheshire Education Committee
1982-87	Governor, Crewe & Alsager College of Higher Education
1982-86	Member of Education Committee, Independent Broadcasting Authority
1983-89	Arts Council Training Committee
1984-87	Executive Committee, Universities Council for Education for Teaching
1986-87	Commission for Racial Equality, Chairman's Research Working Group
1987-94	Chair, Education Committee, Central Television
1987-	Chair of judges – Young Electronic Designer Awards, also Chair of Trustees Young Electronic Designer Awards Governor Design Dimension Project
1987-94	Member of Steering Committee Arts Education for a Multicultural Society – Arts Council/Commonwealth Institute
1987-94	Council, Midland Examination Group
1989-93	Member Steering Committee, Design and Technology Assessment Project – Schools Examination and Assessment Council
1989	Chair, Economic and Social Research Council Conference on Multiethnic Education Research, University of Warwick
1989-93	Consultant Key Stage 3 Standard Attainment

	Test Development Midlands Examination Group
1990-	Member of National Steering Committee of Design and Technology Association
1990-	Vice-Chairman and Chairman of Publishing Committee, Design and Technology Association
1991-94	Member of Education Committee, Design Museum
1993-	Chair – RSA Technology Examination Committee
1995-	Research Adviser – Crafts Council
1997-	RSA Focus Group on Arts in Society, Halifax

Major Research Activities:

1963-67	Research on the Social Environment of Schooling, University of Leicester
1966-1972	Director of Development Project on Design and Craft Education, Schools Council
1968-74	Director of Research Project on the Sociology of the Youth Service, sponsored by the Department of Education and Science
1970-72	Director of the Evaluation study of Project Technology, sponsored by the Schools Council.
1978-80	Director of Research Project, In-service Teacher Education in a Multi-Racial Society, sponsored by the Department of Education and Science
1981-84	Director of Research Project The Educational and Vocational Experiences of Members Ethnic Minority Groups (Eggleston Report)
1981-86	Director, European Workshop on Multi-Cultural Modules for Tertiary Education, Council of Europe

1986-87	Director of research project into Employment of Ethnic Minority Adolescents in Warwickshire.
1985-to date	Director of Evaluation of Technical and Vocational Initiative m Coventry, Warwickshire and Powys (with special interest in multiethnic issues).
1986-88	Director, Ethnic Minority Participants in TVEI Project
1988	Director, Beechdale ESG Evaluation, Walsall LEA
1988-90	Director Education of Unemployed Black Adults Project, Further Education Unit (DES)
1994-	Director, 'Staying on at School' Project. Leverhulme Foundation

Member of Research Advisory Committees including:
Finances of the Youth Service in England and Wales project – Political and Economic Planning Ethnic Relations Research Unit sponsored, by ESRC.

Arts Education for a Multicultural Society sponsored by Gulbenkian Foundation Integrated Studies Curriculum Project, sponsored by the Schools Council

The University of York Enquiry into the Preparation of Teachers for the Socially deprived, sponsored by the Nuffield Foundation

Physics Interface Project sponsored by the Nuffield Foundation

He had **External Examinership** in most British and Irish Universities and many overseas universities m Australia, Barbados, Botswana, Canada, Hong Kong, Jamaica, Malaysia, Singapore, Trinidad, USA.

Major European Activities
1969-1984 – Editor in Chief and subsequently Chairman of Editorial Board of *European Journal of Education*. Ex Officio member of Council of European Institute of Education.

Consultant to a range of major projects of OECD involving field visits to Australia and various European countries, and rapporteur of OECD conferences in 1974 and 1977 also Council of Europe conferences and UK Representative on Working Parties on Post-secondary Education in

Europe for Council of Europe 1972-77 and until 1995 Chairman, Council of Europe Working Party on Intercultural Issues m Higher Education. meeting in UK, Switzerland. France and Malta 1980-86.

Represented OECD at Finnish government National Conference on Educational Development.

Consultant Gibraltar Government Education Department 1981-82

Visiting Professorships: Finland (British Council). University of Turku; Institute of Educational Research, Jyvaskyla; Abo Academy Vasa. Spring 1980; Thessaloniki (British Council) Spring 1986 and Spring 1990

Member – Executive Committee, World Conference of Design and Technology Associations, 1993-

Among his **Major International Activities Outside Europe**, were 1967, 1975, and 1986 Visiting Lecturer in the United States at the Universities of Yale, Boston, Washington Ann Arbor, West Virginia, Maryland.

1973 and 1975 Awarded Visiting Commonwealth Fellowship, Canada and tonight in the Universities of Calgary, Alberta and Lethbridge.

1973 Joint Convenor/Chairruan of International Conference of Design Education. Joint Editor of Conference Report.

1974-76, 1980 and 84 Visiting lecturer in Education at University of Malaysia; University of Science, Malaysia; Pertanian University, Malaysia, Singapore and Colombo.

1975 Chairman, Sociology section, International Comparative Education Society Annual Convention, San Fransisco.

1980, 1984 and 1990 Visiting lecturer Australia and New Zealand at Universities of New England, Macquarie, Monash, Melbourne, Massey, Queensland, Bendigo College of Advanced Education; Ballarat College of Advanced Education; Adelaide College of the Arts and Education and Torrens College

1986 Visiting lecturer, University of the West Indies Barbados and Trinidad,and Curriculum Examinations Council

He also worked in Jamaica and Mexico, and was Visiting Professor, University of Washington, Seattle in 1991, Visiting Professor and Assessor, University of Botswana, Gaborone in 1993, then Consultant in Design and Technology – Ministry of Education, Botswana in 1997

EDITORSHIPS

Editor in Chief of *Paedagogica Europeaca* subsequently *European Journal of Education* 1969-75 published by Council of Europe and European Cultural Foundation – Appointed Chairman of Editorial Board, 1975-85

Editor of *Studies in Design Education. Craft & Technology*, 1968-1995 (relaunched in 1990 *Design & Technology Teaching)*

Chairman of the Editorial Board of the *Sociological Review*, 1970-1982; joint Editor 1982

He was a Member of the Editorial Board of the following journals;
The British Journal of Educational Studies, 1972-1979,
British Journal of Education and Work, 1986-
British Journal of Sociology of Education, 1980-
European Journal of Intercultural Studies, 1989-

Chairman of the Editorial Board of *The International Journal of Design and Technology Education* 1988- and founding Chairman of the Editorial Board of *Multicultural Teaching*, 1982- He was also General Editor of the series of books *The Changing Classroom* for Open Books, Academic Adviser (education) to Routledge and Kegan Paul, Consulting Editor of *New Education* 1978- and *Educational Analysis* 1979-1983 and general Editor of the series of books *The Contemporary Sociology of the School,* Methuen

PUBLICATIONS:
Books

The Social Context of the School, Routledge and Kegan Paul London, 1967, reprinted 1974

Contemporary Research in the Sociology of Education (ed) Methuen, London, 1974 reprinted 1976

Adolescence and Community, E Arnold, London, 1976

Developments in Design Education, Open Books, London 1976 with G N Brown, *Towards an Education for the 21st. Century,* University of Keele, 1970

The Sociology of the School Curriculum, Routledge and Kegan Paul, London, 1977 reprinted 1981

The Ecology of the School, Methuen, London 1977

Experimental Education for Pupils Aged 10-14, (ed), Swetts, The Hague, 1977

Initial and Continuing Training of Teachers. New Trends and Concepts, Mannar, Buenos Aires, 1978

Decision Making in the Classroom, (ed) Routledge and Kegan Paul, London, 1979

School Based Curriculum Development, (ed), Routledge and Kegan Paul, 1980

Work Experience in Secondary Schools, (ed) Routledge and Kegan Paul, London, 1982

with D Dunn, M Anjali and C Wright, *Education for Some,* Trentham Books, 1986 reprinted 1987

with E Sadler, *The Experience of Ethnic Minority Pupils in TVEI*, The Training Agency, Sheffield 1989

Delivering the Technology Curriculum: Six case studies in primary and secondary schools, Trentham Books, 1990

The Challenge for Teachers, Cassell, London, 1993

Teaching Design and Technology, Open University Press, Milton Keynes, 1993, Second Edition 1996

with H Lashley, A Kaur and S Shar *Re-education for Employment,* Trentham Books, 1993

Arts Education in a Multicultural Society, Arts Council/Trentham Books, Stoke-on-Trent, 1996

with G Klein, *Achieving Publication in Education*, Warwick University/ Trentham Books, 1997

Staying on at School – the hidden curriculum of selection, Trentham Books, 2000

Editor of *Teaching and Learning Design and Technology and its Applications – a guide to recent research*, Continuum, 2000

Teaching Design and Technology Third [extensively revised] Edition, Open University Press

He contributed chapters to at least 22 other books and journal contributions began with 'Secondary Schools and 'Oxbridge Blues', *British Journal of Sociology*, in 1965, and continued until 2000.

IN MEMORIAM

Obituaries

Obituaries for John Eggleston appeared in *The Times* (26 December 2001), *The Guardian* (3 January 2002) and *The Independent* (12 January 2002) and in numerous other journals. These include *The Times Educational Supplement, The Bookseller, Sociological Review, Improving Schools, Multicultural Teaching, Design and Technology Teaching.* There follows the obituary from *Improving Schools* vol 5 no 1, 2002.

(Samuel) John Eggleston 11.11.1926-12.12.2001

John Eggleston has died but he will be long remembered. It is difficult to measure the enormous contribution he made to the lives and careers of others, as testified by the tributes which poured in to him during his brief illness. But he is recognised for the enduring and wide-ranging legacies he leaves to education: the theorising of statutory age education, the transformation of Design and Technology, the a raft of highly influential writings, the publishing company committed to social justice.

Born in 1926 in Dorset to an Irish mother and a father traumatised in the Great War, he chose to become a woodwork teacher rather than a carpenter when he left Bath Grammar School. He moved on to become a teacher educator at Loughborough and then Leicester Universities, achieving a BSc(Econ) at LSE.

Through his notable Schools Council project in the late 1960s, John transformed the school subject of Handicraft by liberating children from slavishly reproducing the designs of their teachers and allowing them instead to realise their own ideas and make projects which met their own needs. This revolution formed the basis of Design and Technology as it is today. Sharing his enthusiasm generously and wisely, he edited a journal on Design and Technology for 22 years, co-founded (1987) and chaired the judges of the Young Electronic Designer of the Year Award, and was vice-chair of the Design and Technology Association. Two new books by John on Design and Technology appeared in 2001.

As Professor and head of the Education Department at Keele University (1977-1984), John brought style, intellectual rigour and enterprise to the emerging field of sociology of education. He had a vision of teacher education which went far beyond the current approach and set himself and the talented staff he gathered tough research and publishing standards.

As Professor of Education at University of Warwick from 1985 to 1996, he chaired the education department for seven years. He was awarded honorary doctorates by Middlesex and Sunderland and was an active and involved Visiting Professor at both Central England and Middlesex universities. From the mid-60s to the end of the 90s, he advised a range of educational and government bodies in the UK and also overseas governments and universities.

John had two principles which shaped his career – and his life. Among the 21 books he wrote, *The Ecology of the School* (1977) and *The Challenge for Teachers* (1992) encapsulate the first: the belief that children, like teachers and all adults, need to be 'inner-directed' and not 'other-directed'. John lived and worked according to this principle, treating his academic and publishing colleagues as equals, whatever his status. He never forgot his humble origins and his vigour was tempered by unfailing good humour and a total lack of pretention.

John's second abiding principle was that all children, not just a privileged few, deserve the best possible education. This is reflected in his writing and teaching, but also in his publishing career. He began as a consultant to Methuen and then Routledge and, with his partner Gillian Klein, developed Trentham Books, which has grown steadily since the mid-1980s, consistently promoting social justice in its books and journals. Though he worked frequently for the

Education department over the years, he did not allow the government to suppress the Eggleston Report, which it had commissioned along with the Swann report, as it tried to do when it saw the evidence on its pages of racial discrimination in schools. He published this study of the inequitable career guidance and opportunities offered to ethnic minority 15-18 year-olds through Trentham in 1986, entitling it *Education for Some*.

Design and Technology, the theorising of statutory age education, a raft of highly influential writings, publishing – these are all fields in which John leaves enduring legacies. More difficult to measure is the enormous contribution that he made to the lives and careers of others, as the tributes which poured in to him during his brief illness testify. He will be remembered by many with affection and gratitude.

Gillian Klein

A fuller account of John's contribution to Design and Technology came from *Professor Richard Tufnell*, Dean of Lifelong Learning and Pro Vice-Chancellor of Middlesex University:

John Eggleston was one of a select group of educationalists who have fundamentally changed the educational experience of all our children. This he achieved in what was for long the cinderella subject of the school curriculum, handicraft, by initiating the process which saw this skill-based activity evolve into Design and Technology, a subject now central to every child's education. For it was John who introduced the process of design into the handicraft syllabus of secondary schools in the 1960s. Capturing the mood of the time, this innovation liberated children from slavishly having to reproduce the plans of their teachers and gave them the opportunity to realise their own ideas, and to design and make products which met their needs and desires and not those of their teachers.

By leading the Schools Council 'Design and Making through Craft' project based at Keele University in the late 60s and early 70s, John's team developed both the practical tools and curriculum resources which enabled teachers to bring about this revolution, and the underlying philosophy and rationale which underpinned the subject's evolution for the remainder of the 20th century. His academic rigour and persuasive logic was key to convincing sceptics at all levels that the subject's survival was dependent on fostering children's imagination and creativity, ensuring that minds were just as active as hands in practical lessons. In the 30 years since the project, John has been at the forefront and involved in every aspect of the subject's evolution, sharing his passion and enthusiasm generously and wisely.

All those who are enjoying success through Design and Technology are indebted to John's vision. Young people who are reaping the personal rewards of designing and making new products, aids for the disabled or educational resources for children; teachers who are enjoying motivating careers because they can now harness the energy and creativity of their pupils; and the academic communities whose research activities focused on practical education are now legitimised. The introduction of practically based project work which is both relevant and realistic to the lives of young people will be John's enduring legacy.

The Last Award

John Eggleston was too ill to attend the ceremony in London on 20 November 2001 for his final award – a Fellowship of the City and Guilds of London Institute. Lady Garden, Fellowship Consultant of City and Guilds, made the journey to Stratford on Avon a week later, to present him with his diploma. 'The vast contribution John Eggleston has made to Design and Technology deserves this recognition', she said. 'I was so pleased to be able to represent the Institute and to have the personal pleasure of meeting John.' For John it was a remarkable highlight of his last weeks, from which he drew much pleasure. He listened while Sue Garden read out the citation:

> *For eminence in the field of education, which began with City and Guilds teaching qualifications in Woodwork, Metalwork and Carpentry, followed by a scholarship to the London School of Economics and positions of increasing responsibility in schools, colleges and universities.*

> *He was Professor of Education successively at the universities of Keele and Warwick, heading departments which grew in size*

and standing; he has lectured internationally; his many publications include works which have had a profound influence on every facet of education, with his ideas and advice being both sought and implemented by government. His many services to the community include work on racial equality, the youth service, and teaching quality. He is held in the highest esteem not only by his peers but by many high-flying students and staff who acknowledge his influence in the success of their careers.

For outstanding personal and professional achievement and in recognition of a lifetime contribution to practical education, Fellowship of City and Guilds is awarded to Professor John Eggleston.

Memorial Lecture

The John Eggleston Memorial Lecture for 2003 was featured at the DATA International Research Conference in summer 2003 and is published in *The Journal of Design and Technology Education* vol 8 no3. The title was 'Design matters, and so does philosophy of design' and it was given by Dr Marc J. de Vries of Eindhoven University of Technology, The Netherlands.

Tributes

John Eggleston's personal contributions to the field of education speak for themselves in these pages. So do some of his achievements. But what is missing is the feelings of those who knew him personally, and this brief section is intended to share a few of the most typical letters written firstly to John and then, after his death, in condolence and reminiscence.

John lived for less than three months after the diagnosis of terminal cancer. In that time letters poured in to him in Stratford on Avon.

It is at times like this that you begin to realise the effect that so many 'significant others' have had on your own career and life's work and you realise the debt you owe them.

This from George Shield, who went on:

Your initial influence hit me way back in 1960 or '61 when you first arrived at Loughborogh and began your work with us. What struck me was that you were the first 'handicraft' teacher I knew who had cracked the 'academic' barrier and become a recognised expert in areas other than those of the artisan.

As he began to climb to an academic ladder, he admits to 'shamelessly drawing extensively upon your writings' but it was not until he was studying for the Masters degree that 'you significantly affected my life when you published my first article'.

Another professor who began under John's leadership, Iram Siraj-Blatchford, wrote:

...for me you were, and are, up there with the good and the great. It's been a great privilege that you have bothered with John and me as friends. It will probably embarrass you but you are the closest person I've ever had to a 'father-figure'. I've always been able to rely on you for advice, support and a heart-to-heart when I've most needed it.

Alan Younger wrote:

Your influence has stimulated many professionals to think more positively and deeply about their role and contribution to a generation's education, much to the benefit of a whole cohort of pupils. A true inspiration to not only myself but many others all the way back to your salad days at Loughborough. Thank you for the help and care in my life and career.

And his wife Lesley adds:

You are one of those special people who make others feel as though they too can achieve.

There are several lifetimes' achievements under the Eggleston belt, and I still marvel at how you have managed to fit everything in. Bob Jackson

One of Trentham's authors, Diane Duncan, summed up the feelings of several whom we published for the first time:

I shall always owe John a great deal for believing in my ideas sufficiently to want to publish them.

Later came the letters to Gillian – over 200, making replying [while also resurrecting Trentham] impossible.

John von Knorring, President of Stylus, Trentham's distributor in the US, wrote:

I knew of John Eggleston long before I met him – and the fact that our lives crossed so much later was one of life's great serendipities.

In 1976 I became Marketing Director for what was then Methuen and Co. John had published with Methuen for some years, and was often referred to at editorial board meetings in his capacity as peer reviewer of book proposals we considered. I can to this day remember John Naylor, then Managing Director, quoting him as an irrefutable authority – and as a result I held John Eggleston somewhat in awe, but we never met. He was also editor of the ground-breaking *Contemporary Sociology of the School* series, and we published his *The Ecology of the School* the year before I left for the USA to set up what in due course became Routledge, New York.

Despite our distributing John's book and series in America for many years, we failed to meet. It was not until I left Routledge in 1995 that fate threw us together. In early 1996 I was in the throes of setting up my own company, Stylus Publishing, and visited London looking for educational publishers to distribute in the US.

I still remember with surprise and gratitude that, as a result of that meeting and a proposal I sent a few weeks later, months before my business had opened its doors, that you and John took a gamble and signed on. In retrospect, I think that had a lot to do with John's willingness to take risks and eschew the conventional.

It was after that, on my bi-annual trips to London to visit my British publishing clients, that I got to know John and you, and grew fond of his company, his self-effacing manner, his ever-present humour, and sometimes wicked, but never belittling or sarcastic, observations about both others and himself. While never pushing himself forward, John was always a presence – but a quiet one. He had a twinkling personality, great courtesy and warmth but was also very private. He never talked of his achievements or made any reference, however oblique, to his role in national educational policy. I only learned of all this from you, mostly after his death. Instead we talked publishing, books and politics – on which we shared very similar views – at length over coffee and biscuits.

Meeting with John and you in Highgate twice a year was always, and remains, one of the highlights of my London visits; and I always arranged, as I still do, for ample time for our Trentham get-togethers because they came to be as much an enjoyable social event as a time to discuss business. Though now absent when I visit Trentham, John is still somehow very present. His legacy at Trentham is not just his vision but the sense of integrity, social responsibility and loyalty to staff that he and you embodied, and that you continue to exemplify. These standards and values are rare in publishing today, and are an example that I hope I will always emulate.

As I write this I have in front of me a slightly dog-eared and treasured copy of *The Ecology of the School* – a gift from you – and am looking at John's photo on the back cover: long black hair and side-burns, and heavy black-framed glasses. I never knew him then. The John I knew was white-haired and very distinguished. What my memories and the photo have in common are his piecing eyes, ready smile and expressive eyebrows. I miss him a great deal, and treasure having known him. It amazes me that, although cumulatively I perhaps met John for no more than twenty-four hours in all over six years, that the impression he made was so strong, lasting and full of warmth.

Sir Peter Newsam recalls a trip he and John made together to Japan:

> ...he was utterly at home – or seemed so – there and had an immediate rapport with the people we met. The whole inner-directedness idea, when inessentials are stripped away, was common ground between John and some of the Japanese we met'

and Sir Peter mourns

> ...an academic exceptional in so many ways, practical and theoretical, leaving a large, unfilled gap behind him – but also, as the information from Trentham says, 'vast achievements', of which you and others must be very proud.

A Trentham author and dear friend, Robin Richardson, wrote:

> *I shall always remember John's kindness, cheerfulness, friendliness, and his calm delight in* la comédie humaine. *And the remarkable, the extraordinary creation with you of Trentham Books and all that the two of you did together to change, really change, the world.*

Professor Peter Mortimore's letter of condolence carries the message of this memorial book:

> *...he achieved so much in his life. We should celebrate the life of a person rather than only mourning their passing. In that spirit, let me say – well done, John. We are thinking of you.*